LIBRARY OF CONGRESS

European Collections

AN ILLUSTRATED GUIDE

LIBRARY OF CONGRESS WASHINGTON 1995

This publication was made possible by generous support from the James Madison Council, a national, private-sector advisory council dedicated to helping the Library of Congress share its unique resources with the nation and the world.

The text is composed in Centaur, a typeface designed by American typographer and book designer Bruce Rogers (1870 – 1957).

Designers for this guide were Robert Wiser and Laurie Rosenthal, Meadows & Wiser, Washington, D.C.

COVER: Map of Europe from Ortelius, *Theatrum orbis terrarum* (Antwerp, 1570).

LIBRARY OF CONGRESS CATALOGING-IN-PUBLICATION DATA

   Library of Congress.
     Library of Congress European collections : an illustrated guide.
       p.   cm.
    ISBN 0-8444-0841-7
—— —— Copy 3 Z663.26 .E83 1994
     1. Europe —Civilization —Library resources. 2. Library of Congress. European Division. I. Library of Congress. European Division. II. Title.
   D1055.L46 1994
   016.94 —— dc20   94–32368
                                            CIP

For sale by the U.S. Government Printing Office
Superintendent of Documents
Mail Stop: SSOP, Washington, D.C. 20402 – 9328
ISBN 0-16-045289-9

Contents

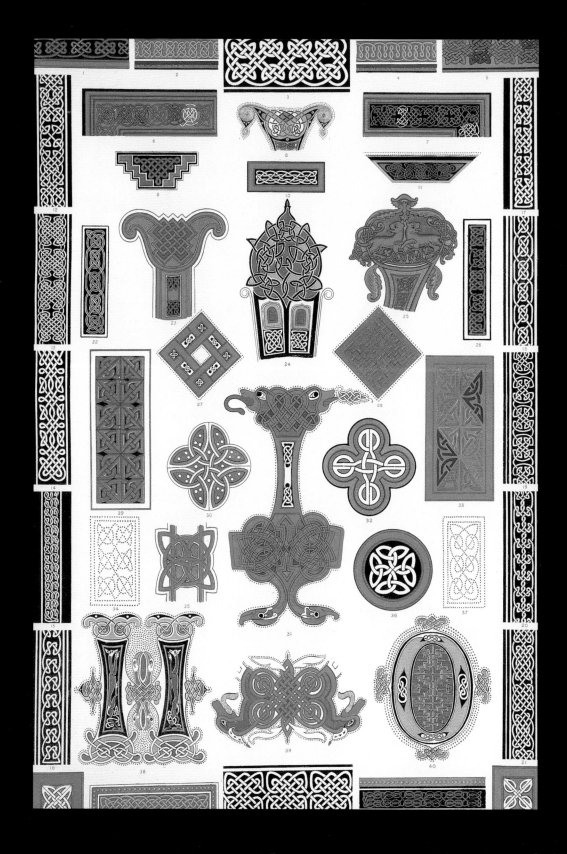

Introduction

In 1814 after the Congress of the United States had lost its library when British soldiers captured Washington and burned the Capitol, former president Thomas Jefferson from his retirement in Monticello offered to replace the lost books by selling to Congress his own library, which was reputed to be the richest private collection in America. Jefferson, who had purchased a sizable portion of his books from dealers in several European cities during his tenure from 1784 to 1789 as minister to France, strongly believed that the involvement of Congress in international as well as national affairs meant that the legislators would benefit substantially from the range of subjects and languages that his collection contained.

Some members, however, challenged the need for such a variety of materials and particularly objected to the French material on both political and moral grounds:

"It might be inferred," said Cyrus King, one of Jefferson's principal antagonists, "from the character of the man who collected it, and France, where the collection was made, that the library contained irreligious and immoral books, works of the French philosophers, who caused and influenced the volcano of the French Revolution which had desolated Europe and extended to this country." Jefferson's books, which would help disseminate his "infidel philosophy," were "good, bad, and indifferent, old, new, and worthless, in languages which many can not read, and most ought not." (Cited in William Dawson Johnston's History of the Library of Congress, *vol. 1, 1800–1864 [Washington: Library of Congress, 1904], 86.)*

King's arguments failed to persuade a majority of his congressional colleagues, and Jefferson's internationalist philosophy has continued to guide collection development at the Library of Congress. Indeed, books, periodicals, maps, prints, manuscripts, musical scores, films, and other library materials originating from Europe are, after Americana, the most extensive and arguably the most important of the Library's holdings. Although the Library does not have discrete "European collections" in the formal sense, European materials are abundant and, in some special fields predominant, among the holdings.

The Library of Congress holds an estimated twenty million book and serial volumes, one-third of which are American imprints. Of the remaining two-thirds, European imprints form a clear majority. And there are areas where European items are especially strong; for example, about 50 percent of the Library's rare books are of European origin. The Library's most valuable book collection, the incunabula, printed with movable type before 1501, is almost exclusively European. This collection of nearly 5,700 books is the largest group of incunabula in the

Owen Jones. *The Grammar of Ornament* (London, 1856). This work, a careful study of Eastern and Western design motifs and a masterpiece of color printing, was one of the books that had an impact on the design of nineteenth-century English furniture and interiors. Plate LXIV is an example of Celtic ornamentation. *(Prints and Photographs Division)*

Letter from Thomas Jefferson, dated October 31, 1823, to the Greek Hellenist and patriot, Adamantios Koraes (here Coray), in which Jefferson responds to Koraes's letter of July 10, 1823, requesting advice on drawing up a constitution for a liberated Greece. (*Manuscript Division*)

Western Hemisphere. In the Geography and Map Division collections, 25 to 30 percent of all maps are European. European countries account for about 96 percent of the documentary materials obtained by the Library's special project of copying foreign manuscripts inaugurated in 1905.

The acquisition of European books and other materials has a long tradition, characterized initially by remarkable individual purchases and donations following the acquisition of Jefferson's collection: the Smithsonian deposit in 1866, the Peter Force library the following year, the purchase in 1904 of the small (1,500 volumes), highly specialized library of the Czech linguist Martin Hattala, the purchase two years later of the 80,000-volume, multilingual library of the renowned Siberian book collector Gennadii Yudin, the receipt on deposit in 1910 of the collection of John Boyd Thacher, and the purchase in 1930 of the Vollbehr Collection.

The Peter Force library launched the Library's collecting of incunabula, and the Yudin acquisition formed the core of the Library's Russian collection. In Hattala's case the purchase provided the Library with its first basic set of key works in Slavic philology. Thacher's deposit, later converted into a gift, contained 904 incunabula. Vollbehr's collection added thousands of incunabula, the most revered being the Library's magnificent Gutenberg Bible.

During the past several decades European materials have been acquired systematically. For most European countries, the Library regulates its supply of currently published books by yearly renewable purchase orders placed with various vendors: national libraries in some cases, private agencies in others. The following statistics illustrate the continual, steady increase of European monographs in the Library's collections: annual additions from Germany, Austria, and Switzerland amount to about 30,000 volumes; French acquisitions total approximately 7,000 volumes yearly; Hungarian monographs increase by about 2,000 volumes every year; the annual rate of acquisition of Czech and Slovak monographs is about 1,500 volumes.

In fact, the Library of Congress holdings of books and other materials from almost all European countries are larger than holdings anywhere else in the world except for the countries themselves. Western and Eastern Europe are equally well represented in the Library of Congress collections. It has been said that items originating from England and Ireland make up the Library's second richest geographic strength. The particularly strong German collections encompass approximately 2.25 million volumes. French items in the general collections are estimated at over one million volumes. Russian-language items amount to about 700,000 volumes, to which may be added about an equal number of volumes in other languages of the former Soviet Union and in Western languages about Russia. Italian items number about 500,000 volumes, and the Spanish collections are of approximately equal size. Poland is represented by about 130,000 books and bound serials.

Jan V. Chełmiński. *L'Armée du duché de Varsovie* (Paris, 1913). Shown here is Prince Poniatowski's aide-de-camp, on one of fifty-two such plates illustrating the glorious, if brief, history of the Army of the Duchy of Warsaw, 1807–15. *(Rare Book and Special Collections Division)*

Surprisingly broad are the collections of some of the smaller European countries. The Dutch and Flemish collections consist of about 180,000 items; works on Hungary and Hungarians or by Hungarian authors amount to about 130,000 items; the Czech and Slovak collections are estimated at more than 100,000 volumes.

In general, the European collections in the Library of Congress are well-balanced, but a few special features do stand out in comparison with the holdings of major libraries in Europe. Owing to its emphasis on materials related to

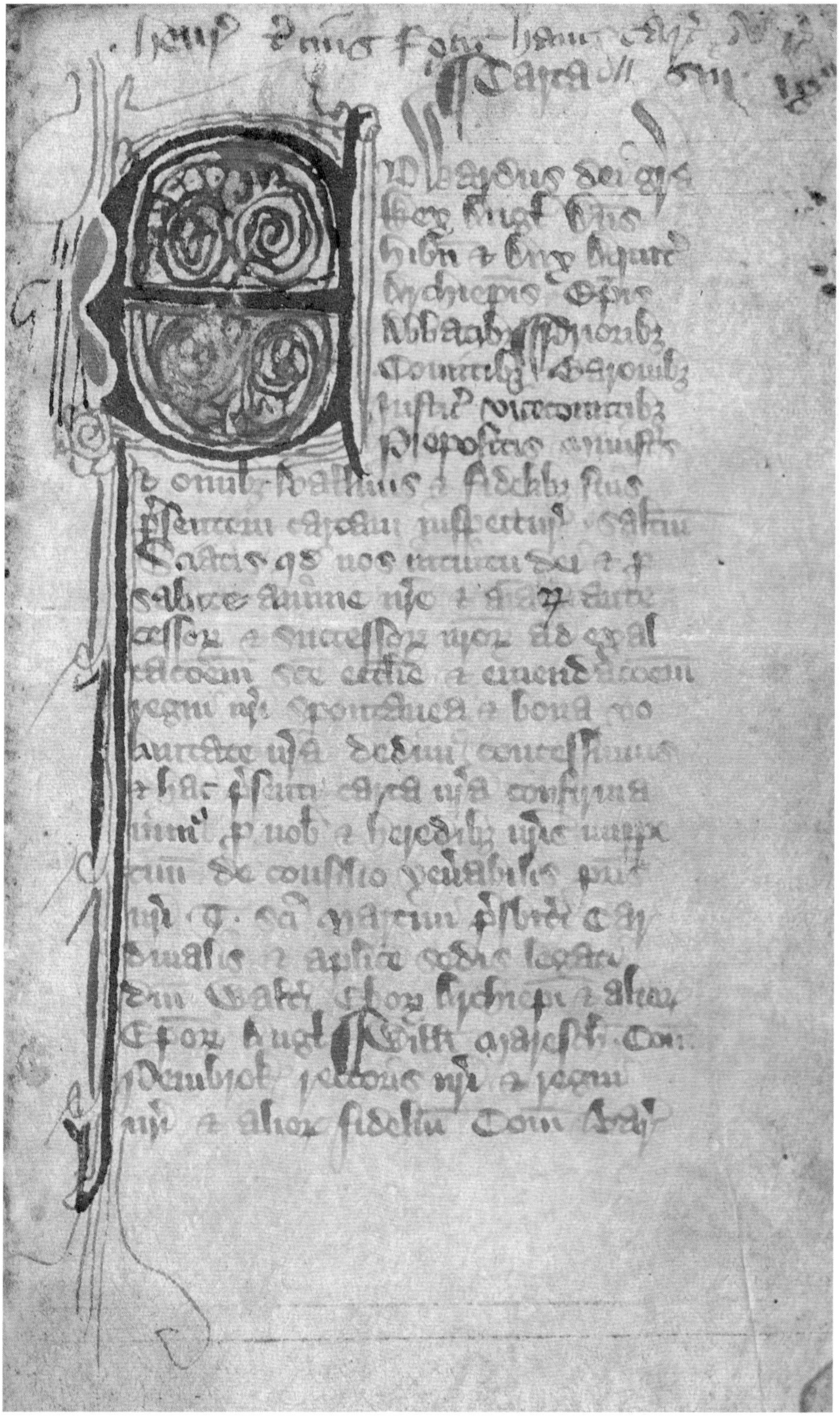

the United States, the Library of Congress has become the world's largest repository of publications and documents that have to do with American-European ties in certain historical periods, including records of European exploration of the New World, genealogical records, and materials describing the experiences of American artists and literary figures in Europe.

Another case of the probably unequaled strength of the Library's European collections is literature temporarily classified as *libri prohibiti*. For many decades the Library collected books and periodicals that were not available to researchers in Central and Eastern Europe under the communist régimes. These include *samizdat* publications, émigré literatures, and works of Western authors on Central and Eastern Europe. For this reason the European collections of the Library of Congress are, in these genres, even more inclusive than the domestic library collections in some of the European countries themselves, such as Russia, Romania, or the Czech Republic.

It is obvious that the influence of literature published in European languages far exceeds the geographical limits of Europe. For example, the significance of the European collections in the Library of Congress is enhanced by the fact that some of the European languages have become standard or literary languages on other continents. French-speaking areas include not only France and parts of Belgium, Luxembourg, and Switzerland but also countries, regions, or social groups in Africa, Asia, North America, and the Middle East. Portuguese is the official language of several African countries and of Brazil, and Spanish is dominant in most of the rest of South and Central America. Russian remains widely spoken in vast territories in Asia outside the Russian Federation. And, of course, the present status of English as the lingua franca of almost the whole world is the best example of linguistic interaction between Europe and other continents.

A variety of format conveys the riches of the European collections of the Library of Congress, including books, manuscripts, letters, maps, drawings, music scores, musical instruments, films, and photographs. European materials reside both in the general collections of the Library and in the special collections. The various formats and types of collections are discussed throughout this volume, but for clarity's sake we begin with sections on the principal subject areas—the humanities and social sciences, the arts, and science and technology—before turning to more detailed discussions of the Library's special collections, its rare books and manuscripts, and its maps. Finally, this guide focuses on a unique strength, the Library's unparalleled materials on European Americana and American Europeana.

The European collections of the Library of Congress are strongest in the hu-

Der Sachsenspiegel (Germany, ca. 1500). A page from the illuminated manuscript of one of the oldest and most influential law codes written in High German during the Holy Roman Empire. The original Sachsenspiegel dates from 1230. *(Rare Book and Special Collections Division)*

9

manities and social sciences, with special strengths in language, literature, history, geography, political science, law, the arts, and economics. Reference materials in all these areas, but particularly in the social sciences and humanities, are represented as comprehensively as possible. For most European countries the Library of Congress offers in-depth coverage of a wide variety of subjects throughout all periods. All in all, the Library provides the best resources in the United States for the study of European affairs in the broad disciplines of social sciences, humanities, and law.

All forms of art are strongly represented in the Library of Congress, but music stands out as the strongest single area with about 600 donor-named collections containing instruments, original scores, manuscripts, librettos, and original recordings, most of which are European in provenance or inspiration. Of course one need only visit the magnificent Main Reading Room of the Library's Thomas Jefferson Building to be reminded of the heritage of European art and architecture at the institution, and the arts section of this guide also outlines the art and architecture catalogs from various centuries and the numerous books illustrated by renowned artists. Noteworthy, in addition, are the Library's extensive holdings of films from several European countries.

For centuries Europe has played a leading role in many areas of science, a fact mirrored in the Library's vast and diverse holdings of scientific and technological literature. From the first complete edition of the works of Archimedes to an original copy of Sir Francis Bacon's *Novum organum* to a complete twenty-eight-volume set of Diderot's *Encyclopédie*, the Library of Congress is a treasure trove, largely centered on Europe, for the historian of science. The Library, of course, acquires a full complement of contemporary scientific and technological journals and holds nearly four million technical reports, including technical standards from France, Germany, Great Britain, Russia, and the European Union.

The many special collections at the Library of Congress include some on individual European countries like Bulgaria, Portugal, and Russia; others on discrete fields of endeavor or knowledge with a strong European accent, like aeronautics, gastronomy, or magic; and still others on individual European personalities.

Breathtaking in their richness and variety, the Library's rare book and manuscript collections feature the Gutenberg Bible, one of only three known complete copies printed on vellum. The Library possesses legal milestones like England's *Magna Charta* and France's *Grand Coutumier de Normandie*, and manuscripts of the *Sachsenspiegel* and of the *Russkaia Pravda*, the oldest law codes of Germany and Eastern Europe, respectively. Rare editions of many European writers,

Magna charta cum statutis angliae (14th c.). Among the Law Library's rarest books, this miniature manuscript (here shown enlarged to reveal detail) is still in its original pigskin wrapper. Very intricate colored pen work graces this small version of the basic source of English common law. *(Law Library, Rare Book Room)*

Vn vernembt vnh der
herrn gepurd von dem
launde zu sachsen
Der von anehald vnd
der von brandenburkh
vnd der von Ole nude
vnd der Marggraf vo
meyssen vnd der graf
von brone dvß furste
sind all swaben Der
von hakchenbozne vn
der von gueyß vnd der
von mathele vnd des
richs schephen dy sind
all swaben Der von
trebulo vnd der von
edelrstorf Hanureich
iudas von suetlinge

der voyt Albrecht vo spo
daw vnd elberith vnd
Conrad von suetlynge
vnd sorappen dimd vnd
reslaue Anne von re
chenstorp herman vo
mernge heydolfes thin
der von vnnigen vnd d
von seedorff dy sind all
swaben dye laundgra
ßen von durmgen sind
frankchen vnd der von
reinstain vnd der von
plankchenburg vnd der
purkhgraf vo werlm
vnd dy von Clodne vnd
der von drolizke vnd dy
von chathebus das sind
alles frankchen dy von
prawnswig vnd dy vo
luuenburg vnd dy von
papenburg vnd dye vo
Osterburg vnd dy vo al
tenhuzen dy sind all swa
ben vnd dy vo wernigen
rode vnd dy von arsteyn
vnd dy vo wesenrode vn
dy von amersleue vnd

CORANT OR VVEEKLY NEVVES,
from Italy, Germany, Hungaria, Polonia, Bohemia,
France, and the Low-Countries.

including Herodotus, Augustine, and Descartes; Burke, Kant, and Lomonosov; and Keats, Goethe, and Dostoyevsky, grace the Library's collections. In 1993, the Library passed a milestone when it acquired its 100,000,001st item, and it was European—the first printed account of the fifteenth-century Portuguese discoveries.

A special pride of the Library of Congress is its splendid collection of maps, which include more than one million items of European cartographic material in virtually every form. They range from a 1474 first edition of Ptolemy's *Gēographikē* and a 1595 first edition of Mercator's *Atlas* to early twentieth-century maps of Europe that played a role at the peace conferences ending World War I.

Perhaps nothing at the Library of Congress is culturally more significant than its unique collection of European Americana and American Europeana. Beginning with the *Columbus Codex (Book of Privileges)* of 1502 and Martin Waldseemüller's *Cosmographiae introductio* of 1507 in which the word "America" appeared in print for the first time, the Library's holdings vividly trace the ties that link the Old and New Worlds. One can find the maps of early European explorers and accounts of the tribulations of the first European settlers. The period of the American Revolution is extensively documented in the Count de Rochambeau Papers, and letters of Revolutionary War advisers Lafayette, von Steuben, Kościuszko, and Pułaski to American founding fathers like Washington, Jefferson, Madison, and Hancock are among the Library's treasures of European Americana.

For the era of the First World War and its aftermath, the Library of Congress offers a multitude of both published works and unique manuscript documents—in the Woodrow Wilson Papers, the Robert Lansing Papers, and elsewhere—illustrating the movements for the independence of Poland, Czechoslovakia, and other countries that have been assisted by the United States. Today, thousands of individual Americans use the impressive genealogical resources of the Library to trace their family roots to Europe. The Library's collections also provide a fascinating array of Americans' perspectives on Europe and of European exiles' poignant views of their homelands from these shores.

✻ ✻ ✻ ✻ ✻

The writing of this book was a team effort, led by the talented area specialists and research librarians of the Library's European Division. Unlike many other units of the Library of Congress, the European Division is not the custodian of most of the materials that support its acquisitions and reference work. Hence, the staff of the division, collectively and individually, visited and consulted with colleagues throughout the Library to assess the particular strengths of the vast holdings on the countries of Europe on which they are expert and for which they are responsible. Most of the division's area specialists and reference librarians wrote lengthy country-specific essays, which have been edited and made available online via Internet. Special thanks are due Carol Armbruster, Ronald Bachman, Grant Harris, Harold Leich, Kenneth Nyirady, and Predrag Pajic for integrating the voluminous findings of the country-specific essays in the writing of first drafts of the textual sections of this guide.

In addition, since the administrative structure of the Library places Spain and Portugal in the Hispanic Division and Great Britain and Ireland in the Humanities and Social Sciences Division, we were aided by specialists from those areas and by experts in the classics and in Hebraica. I am deeply appreciative of their assistance.

Above all, I am indebted to my colleagues David H. Kraus, Assistant Division Chief and Specialist for Eastern Europe, and particularly George Kovtun, Specialist for the Czech Republic, Slovakia, and Eastern Europe. Their indefatigable labors spanned a range of tasks, from research and writing to collating and organizing, to assisting in choosing the illustrations for the book from a great variety of interesting possibilities. They and the other contributors mentioned above, with good humor and deep cultural sensitivity, have collaborated on this volume, which attempts to convey the remarkable breadth and richness of the European collections of the Library of Congress.

MICHAEL H. HALTZEL
CHIEF, EUROPEAN DIVISION

Front page of *Corant or Weekly Newes, from Italy, Germany, Hungaria, Polonia, Bohemia, France, and the Low-Countries*, published in London on October 11, 1621. Acquired with the Feleky Collection of Hungarica in 1953, the *Corant* was at that time the oldest-known extant copy of an English-language newspaper. (*Rare Book and Special Collections Division*)

multo numero argumentoꝛ: ↄ copi-
sum aurū possidere in ea legitur ani-
-na uestra in misericordia eius: et non
ↄfundemini in laude eꝰ. Operamini
opus uestrū āte tempꝰ: ↄ dabit uobis
mercedē uestram in tpe suo Explic liber ecclesiastiꝯ Incipit oꝛo salomonis.
Et idinauit salomon genua sua ɨ
conspectu totius ecclesie irahel:
et aperuit manꝰ suas ad celum
et dixit. Dūe deus irhł nō est tibi similis
deus in celo sursum neqꝫ in terra deoꝛ-
sum: qui custodis testamentū tuū et
misericordiā pueris tuis euntibus in
conspectu tuo in toto corde. Euans pue-
ro tuo dauid que locutꝰ es illi:et locutꝰ es in ore tuo et in manu tua im-

ema uni
uiderit i
rea eoꝛ
breuiꝰ
mi
uel
ut
ri: ut p̄ cola
tiꝫ prola
Hoc q̄ n
interptari
genere
la fuer
luꝛ: er
ga
er

... pretas uersib9
descriptas me-
... mer apud he-
... gari. et aliquid si-
... abere de psalmis
... tibus salomonis.
... uere z tullio solet sie-
... ant et comara: qui u-
... o uersibus conscripserut.
... tan legendu pudentes:
... em nouia nouo scribendi
... nixim9. Ac primu de ysa-
... q in sermone suo disertus
... ut uir nobilis z urbane de-
... ne habes quicqua i eloquio
... ratis amixtu. Vnde accidit:
... re uertis flore suonis ei9 tralla-
... no potuerit obscurare. Deinde eria
... no adiugendu: q no tam prophera
... ur q euangelista. Itaq3 uni-
... uum9 sir q euangelista. ut
... q epi ecclesieq3 misteria ad liqui
... ur q est: ut non eum putes de
... sed de pteritis histo-
... uo noluisse tuc

---

ur z tsta ...
digneut incipia ne uidea ...
sea respiciant ne uidea ...
rio. Sed et non psumptione au ...
tennare. Prophetauit aut ysa ...
iherusale et in iudea necdu uenin au ...
bubus in captiuitatem ducis: ac de ...
unaq3 regno nuc couixi nuc separa ...
eum regit oraculu. Et eum interdu ad
psentem respiciat historia: z post ba-
bilonie captiuitate reditu ppli signifi ...
et in iudeam: tame omnis eius cura
uocatione gentiu et de aduentu
Que quam plus amaris o
euchorpui. tanto magis ab eo
ur p obnuciatione pleniu qua
sineuter emuli lauiat ipe in
uem restituar in futuro:
hoc in pegrine lingu ...
uasse. ne iudei de ...
rum ecclesiis eius ...

Explic plog ...

iudei

M aterials in the various disciplines of the social sciences and humanities in all formats form in a very real sense the heart of the European collections of the Library of Congress. The Library's holdings include printed materials from the first printed book, the Gutenberg Bible of 1454–55, up to the most recent issues of newspapers describing the current events of the day—whether of local or world importance—recording the turmoil caused by the reunification of Germany, the emergence of democracy in the former communist countries of Eastern Europe and the former Soviet Union, the war in Bosnia, and the latest developments in the economic, political, and social integration of the European Union.

The European social science and humanities collections relate to all periods of civilization and history, beginning from the very dawn of European culture in the Stone Age as reported in the archaeological literature, and continuing through the great classical civilizations of Greece and Rome up to the present. In addition to print media, the Library collects social science and humanities materials in sound recordings, motion pictures, photographs, prints, maps, and other formats.

The classics were strongly represented both in the original Library of Congress collection and in Jefferson's library that replaced the volumes burned. In fact, one can even see Mr. Jefferson's handwritten corrections in the margins of Greek and Latin works that he sold to the Library. Today the holdings in the classics of the Library of Congress rank among those of major importance in the United States. A vast array of materials that range from texts of classical authors, translations, commentaries, and historical discussions to excavation reports and reference works to collections of inscriptions, vases, and sculptures is found in the Library's general collections. Latin, Greek, and other ancient language manuscripts from the Armenian Patriarchate of Jerusalem, various monasteries of Mount Athos, and the Monastery of Saint Catherine on Mount Sinai can be consulted on microfilm in the Microform Reading Room.

An examination of many early imprints in Latin and Greek, early translations, and historical discussions housed in the Rare Book and Special Collections Division can lead to serendipitous discoveries of early printed travel accounts with drawings of now-destroyed ancient monuments or prints in early works published in one area and then used again by newly founded printing houses thousands of miles away. Justifiably famous is the Library's antique map collection, which will be discussed in the Maps section below. The Law Library holds major collections of Roman law and canon law, and the Prints and Photographs Division collec-

PREVIOUS PAGES. A detail from the Gutenberg Bible (Mainz, 1454–55), the first book printed with movable type. The Library of Congress copy, acquired in 1930 as part of the Vollbehr Collection of incunabula, is one of three perfect vellum copies of the Gutenberg Bible. (*Rare Book and Special Collections Division*)

OPPOSITE. Comte Alexandre de Laborde. *Fragmens d'une Mosaïque découverte à Tarragone,* 1802, a hand-colored aquatint. From his *Description d'un pavé en mosaïque découvert dans l'ancienne ville d'Italica* (Paris, 1802). This illustration of a mosaic pavement in Tarragona in northwestern Spain is from a rare volume of one of the great archaeological documentation publishing projects of the early nineteenth century. (*Rare Book and Special Collections Division*)

tions include numerous photographs and lithographs of ancient monuments.

Taking current European countries as a reference point, one learns that in virtually every case the Library's social science and humanities collections are the largest in North America, and at the same time the largest outside the country of origin. Thus, for example, the Library has the largest collection of materials from Spain and relating to matters Spanish outside of Spain itself. The same is true for most of the Eastern European countries and Russia. The Russian collections taken as a whole represent the largest single concentration of Russian materials outside the major repositories of Moscow and Saint Petersburg.

Owing to the preeminence of Europe in world affairs between the age of exploration beginning in the fifteenth century and the colonization and settlement of most of the world by European powers, the Library's European collections in the social sciences and humanities are, in effect, worldwide in scope and focus, but at the same time, they are intensely and deliberately national. The collections reflect each European nation's distinctive history, literature, culture, religion, geography, and civilization. The Library collects not only from and about the largest states of Europe—France, Germany, Italy, Russia, Ukraine, and the United Kingdom—but also from and relating to smaller ones such as Denmark, Latvia, Luxembourg, Malta, Portugal, and Slovenia. Moreover, it collects materials by and about minority nationalities and ethnic groups that do not form independent countries—the Basques of France and Spain, the Frisians of Holland and Germany, the Romansh speakers of Switzerland, the Wends of Germany, the Vlachs of the Balkan Peninsula.

Because of wars, revolutions, and general political turmoil in Europe over the past several centuries, large numbers of people frequently have emigrated or been exiled from their homelands and obliged to settle elsewhere on the continent or around the world. Publications of these groups provide an important and essential counterbalance to official materials—often expressing a narrowly "party-line" position—from the home country.

This role of émigré publications holds particularly true for the countries of the former Soviet Union and Eastern Europe, which were ruled by communist governments for many decades, until the late 1980s and early 1990s, and where governments tightly controlled publishing and censored much original research and publication in politically sensitive areas such as history, literary criticism, and political science. The same situation applied in Spain and Portugal until their self-liberation from fascism in the 1970s.

At the core of the Library's European social science and humanities collec-

Hartmann Schedel. *Liber chronicarum* (Nuremberg, 1493). The Nuremberg Chronicle, the most heavily illustrated book from the late fifteenth century, is a history of the world told with a mixture of biblical, mythological, and historical themes. Illustration no. 290 shows the artist's conception of Portugal. *(Lessing J. Rosenwald Collection, Rare Book and Special Collections Division)*

Portugalia

In portugalia petrus agnomine ïnfans.ſic eꝰ ſilij regis anteꝗ regnant appellanꞇ .magni nominis prī/
ceps qui totam ferme europam peragrauerat ſue virtutis documenta demonſtrans.Cum regnum tuto
rio nomïe aliꝗdiu ſumma cum laude adminiſtraſſet nec minoꝛe fide alphonſo ex fratre nepoti ſimul ꞇ gene
ro ſuo reſtituïſſet.tandē ſubꝛotis ytrimꝗ diſſenſionibus cum odio creſcente ad plïum ventum eſſet ſagitta in
incertū miſſa tranſfixus interijt.vir magnoꝛ operū.Et qui olim ſub ceſare ſigiſmundo ſtipendia faciens nõ
paruā ſibi gloꝛiam in turchos pugnando parauerat.Alfonſus exinde manſuetiſſimus pꝛinceps alti coꝛdis
et pꝛudentia.ſingulari pditus neꝗ eū vnꝗ regius portugalia ſanguis deriuatus eſt.poſt hec regnum quie/
te tenuit.cui cū obijſſet dilectiſſima pïunx.eademꝗ ſoꝛoꝛ patruelis yt aliam ſupduceret ſuaderi non potuit.
ſed omnis eius cura eo conuerſa eſt yt aliquid agat quod ſibi laudem ꞇ xpiane religioni fructū pariat.Qua
pꝛopter inuitatis regni pꝛoceribus ſuſcepto publice crucis ſigno claſſem in turchos ꞇ expeditionem pmiſit
Annis vo ſequentibus heinricus infans videns regni portigalie fines paruis limitibꝰ contineri cupiēs re
gnū ápliare occeanū hiſpanicū ſummis viribꝰ igredit ſuaſu ꞇ doctrina coſmographoꝛ ſiꞇ terre ꞇ mari noſcē
cū.inuētiꝗ multis ꞇ varijs inſulis ab hoïbꝰ nūcꝗ habitat.Inter ceteras pclara inſulã nõ ſine ſuoꝛ letitia
adnauigat.nõ tamen hominibꝰ habitatā ſed fontibus irriguam pïngui gleba refertam nemoꝛoſam.incolē
dis honibꝰ aptā.ad quā diuerſa hominū genera colendā imiſit.Inter tñ ceteros fructꝰ aptiſſima ē ad.pcre
andū zuccaꝛ.ꝗ tanto fenoꝛe ibi nūc cõficiꞇ yt vniuerſa europa zuccaro plꝰ ſolito habūdet.nome inſule ma

LA BIBLE,

Qui est toute la Saincte Escripture contenant le Vieil & Nouueau Testament, ou Alliance.

Essaie. I.
Escoutez cieulx, & toy terre preste l'oreille: car l'Eternel parle.

L'Oliuier de Robert Estienne.

M. D. LIII.

tions lie the thousands of general periodicals and journals and the holdings of reference sources that provide general information, assistance, and specific guidance in using the published literature. For most European countries, the general periodical collections are remarkably complete and include scholarly and literary journals, current-events and news magazines, major daily and weekly newspapers, and the serial publications and transaction journals of learned societies, institutes, and other research centers. The reference collections include encyclopedias, dictionaries, handbooks, directories, bibliographies, biographical sources, gazetteers, atlases, catalogs, and general surveys and guides to countries, subjects, time periods, personalities, and groups.

In history and the other social sciences, the Library has comprehensive collections allowing researchers to study every European country and nationality from the earliest times to the present. As with periodicals, the Library's collections are particularly strong in published primary source documents, often issued serially or in large sets by each country's major research centers and producers of scholarship—the academies, universities, colleges, learned societies and associations, libraries, museums, archives, and the like.

All aspects of history are covered in the European collections, including political, social, cultural, and labor history, as well as biographical literature and the histories of individual disciplines—the history of science, for example. In addition to primary published source documentation, the Library attempts to collect all major secondary historical and historiographical scholarship and, very selectively, popular writings on history.

All periods of European history are well represented, but the history collections are most comprehensive and complete for modern Europe—the age of exploration and colonization in the fifteenth and sixteenth centuries, the Renaissance and Reformation, the rise of empires, the beginning of the development of

Van der Linde. *Leven en daden van Johannes Sobietzki de III . . .* (Amsterdam, 1685). This handsome engraving depicts the military hero and future Polish king, Jan III Sobieski, who in 1683 defeated the Turks at Vienna. *(Rare Book and Special Collections Division)*

OPPOSITE. La Bible. ([Geneva], 1553). The Geneva revision is the first Protestant French Bible. *(Bible Collection, Rare Book and Special Collections Division)*

national self-identity and consciousness, the period of major revolutions and wars—the French Revolution, 1848, the two world wars, the Russian Revolution—the Cold War, and, finally, the period of East European democratization, the fall of communism, and the development and enlargement of the European Union. For the past twenty years the Library has videotapes of television news broadcasts and documentary films from a number of European countries, including France, Germany, Italy, Poland, the former Yugoslavia, and Russia, to supplement other documentary sources and print materials.

Other disciplines that are critical for historical research—archaeology, paleography, genealogy, numismatics, heraldry, chronology—are well represented. From around the world, the Library collects comprehensively materials on archives and archival holdings relating to Europe and European nationalities.

In the related areas of political science, foreign relations, and law, the Library's European collections emphasize primary source documents such as the minutes of parliamentary meetings and debates, official government gazettes that record decrees and regulations, treaties, laws, court decisions and rulings, and commentaries on legal texts. Holdings in the collections reflect the development of democracy and representative government, beginning in Ancient Greece and continuing through its reemergence in the age of the democratic revolutions. They document its twentieth-century collapse into authoritarianism and totalitarianism in many European countries, up to the restoration of democracy in post-Franco Spain and post-Salazar Portugal in the 1970s and in most of the formerly communist countries of Eastern Europe in the early 1990s.

Geography and travel are amply represented in the Library's collections. Maps and other cartographic materials form the true core of the geography collection, but the Library also comprehensively collects book materials on descriptive, physical, cultural, and social geography. Such materials include travel accounts from the early medieval period to the present, scholarly journals, and individual studies, monographs, and conference reports on geographical topics relating to Europe.

Similarly, publications in the fields of economics, demography, and statistics are strongly represented in the Library's European collections. The economics collection includes all major works in theoretical and practical economics. Works on business and commerce are particularly well represented for the twentieth century, and the Library has a virtually complete collection—in print form or microform—of all statistical yearbooks, census reports and results, and more specialized studies published by every European state.

OPPOSITE LEFT. *Vanity Fair Album* (London, 1876). Displayed in the album are very fine caricatures of important personages of the day. The Duke of Connaught, Queen Victoria's third son, is described by the editors as "quite unspoilt, and though now over six-and-twenty his morals are held to be still above all reproach." *(Prints and Photographs Division)*

OPPOSITE RIGHT. Norbert Goeneutte. *Octobre, 1880,* a photogravure. From *L'Art de la mode,* vol. 1 (1880–81), facing p. 72. A typical fashion plate from this influential fashion magazine of the French Third Republic. *(Prints and Photographs Division)*

קונדמאבונג

די פארשטעהער דער לעמבערגער איזראעליטישן געמינדע מאכן
בעקאנט לכל בני ישראל אינגאליציען קראקא אונד דר בוקאווינא
דאס די פריפונג ביי דעם רבייאמט וועגן דער היראטס
בעװיליגונג העדט שון אויף :

דעם רבייאמט העדט גאן אויף . נאר	קױרליך געװען אין ניװיארק
װער עס װיל היראטן בדארף גיבט	כלהמון פר דר התונה זיך אב פריױן
מעהר נאר איין ציגניס פאן דערשולע	ביי דעם רבייאמט דאס זיא קענען
דאס ער האט אינדר שולע גלערנט	דייטש לעזן אונד שרײבן אונד רעכנן
ארער דאס ער האט זיך אב גיפריואט	אונד די צעהן געבאט אונד נאך אנדרע
גלערנט אונד האט זיך אך גיפריואט	זאכן אויסדעם ביכל בני ציון . האבן
דער שולע . אונד איין ציגניס פאן דעם	זיא אבר דיא פריאונג גמאכט איזט
רב אדר פאן דעם רעליגיאנסווייזר	נאר קינע מענליכקײט גומען אויף דר
דאס ער האט דיא רעליגיאן אין	היראטס בעװיליגונג אײנצוהרכן . דאס
ביידע ציניסע רײכט ער אין צודעם	עם זיך אײנמאל גטראפן דאס איינר
פארשטעהר פאן איין שטאאט . דער	האט אויף קינען פאל ניכט גקאנט דיא
פארשטעהר איברשיקט עם צו דעם	פריאונג מאכן . האט ערגומוזט דאריבר
רבייאמט . אונד ער בעקומט דיא	צו דער האכן ק׳ ק׳ שטאטהאלטרייא
בעװיליגונג צו היראטן . ער װירד אין	אײנרײכן . דאס יעדרעם קרײאאמט דאם
ארדענטליכר פאמיליאנט לכבוד	האט מיניסטעריום װא גענעדיג געװען
ולתפארת . איין בעל הבית אין דר .	אונד האט אם 20 טען יוניער 1858 צום
געמינדע װיא עסזיך געהרט .—	גוען גמאכט . דאס דיזע פריאונג ביי

The study of society itself is represented by
the disciplines of sociology, anthropology, ethnol-
ogy, and folklore. The Library's collections in
these disciplines are strong, relating to all European nations and groups. Included, for example,
are scholarly studies and monographs, reports of
fieldwork and ethnographic investigations, recordings of folk music, collections of folktales and
epics, and studies related to the theory of society
and its functioning.

The Library has extensive collections on each
of the languages of Europe, both those spoken by
many millions of people, such as English, German,
French, Spanish, Russian, Ukrainian, and Polish,
and the less widely used languages like Welsh, Mal-
tese, Albanian, Latvian, and Estonian. Holdings for
each language include grammars, dictionaries, readers, textbooks for foreigners, and the principal
scholarly histories, commentaries, etymological
treatments, periodicals, bibliographies, and gram-
matical and lexical studies.

European Yiddica, Hebraica, and Ladino are
particularly strongly represented in the Library's
collections. Produced primarily, though not exclusively, in Europe during the nineteenth century, the
Yiddish-language collections include approximately
15,000 monographic titles as well as a comprehensive collection of serials and newspapers. Much
larger are the Library's Hebraic collections, which
contain more than 100,000 titles, ranging from
thousand-year-old rabbinic responses to eigh-
teenth- and nineteenth-century *haskalah* (Jewish En-
lightenment) literature. The Hebraic Section of the
Library's African and Middle Eastern Division
houses a small collection of Hebrew manuscripts as
well as broadsides and other documents that reflect
on Jewish life in Europe. Especially interesting are

Boethius. *De consolatione philosophiae* (Ghent, 1485). This early printed book has many hand-painted illustrations depicting Lady Philosophy and scenes of daily life in fifteenth-century Ghent. *(Lessing J. Rosenwald Collection, Rare Book and Special Collections Division)*

OPPOSITE. A broadside in Yiddish, issued on March 22, 1858, by the representatives of the Jewish community of Lemberg, informs Jews of Galicia, Cracow, and Bukovina that the special test for grooms and brides before their marriage, imposed by royal decree in 1805, has been rescinded by the government. *(Hebraic Section, African and Middle Eastern Division)*

Hebrew newspapers published during the nineteenth century. Approximately 600 Ladino titles, many of which were produced in European cities, are also located in the Hebraic Section.

The Library's collections in general, theoretical, historical, and synchronic linguistics are also robust, particularly in the area of comparative Indo-European linguistics and its various subdisciplines, such as Romance, classical, and Slavic philology. Since the scientific study of language and languages in the modern period had its beginnings in Europe, the Library's European linguistics collections are in fact worldwide in coverage and significance.

The literature collections of the Library of Congress are extremely strong for almost every European country. All European literatures, both of major nations and of smaller ethnic groups, many without their own state, are represented in the Library's collections in the original language and selectively in English translation. The Library collects works of modern literature in various genres—novels, plays, poetry, short stories, and the like—a selection of current authors and popular writers, and materials on the history and criticism of each European literature and of individual European writers. The literature collections in print materials are enhanced by a number of collections of sound recordings, described in the Special Collections section below.

Materials in religion and philosophy are integral to the Library of Congress collections. The four major European religious traditions—Roman Catholicism, Eastern Orthodoxy, Protestantism, and Judaism—are represented not only by the standard editions of basic scriptural and interpretive texts but by a comprehensive selection of commentaries, church histories, polemical and pastoral works, church law and regulations, periodicals, and reference materials. Islam in Europe is also represented, especially by numerous publications on the history and culture of Moorish Spain and the Ottoman Balkans, and, more recently, the Muslim communities in the Balkan countries.

Finally, in the social sciences and humanities, the Library of Congress makes special efforts at collecting European materials in the area of book studies, librarianship, and bibliography. The printed book is, of course, a European invention, and in addition to a number of special collections—such as incunabula, early printed Bibles, and illuminated manuscripts—the Library has strong holdings in materials relating to the history of printing and publishing in each country, the development and current state of libraries and archives, and the field of descriptive and analytical bibliography. Of particular value to scholars are the Library's descriptive materials about the major libraries in each European country.

Gaspare Fossati. *Aya Sofia* (London, 1852). Plate no. 15 from the portfolio of the Italian architect hired to restore the mosque of Aya Sofya in Istanbul in the mid-nineteenth century. This edifice, now serving as a museum, was built in the sixth century as the Christian church of Hagia Sofia. *(Prints and Photographs Division)*

The Arts

European art can be found in the Library of Congress in all possible forms, representing every corner of the continent, and giving a broad picture of the artistic achievements of the peoples of Europe. One can get a bird's-eye view of this diversity by browsing through major European art encyclopedias and countless art books or by listening to and viewing the works of major European artists in music, film, photography, and folk art. Moreover, the European heritage of the founders of the Library is evident in the style of the very building in which many of these treasures have been preserved. With its facade modeled after the Paris Opera House and its Great Hall after the Grand Foyer of the Vienna Opera House, the Library's Jefferson Building could be likened to a jewelry box that is "lined" in the Great Hall, corridors, Main Reading Room, and smaller reading rooms with the decorative work and design of Italian and American artists in the manner of many European palaces.

In view of this architectural setting, it is not surprising that the Library has become a treasure house of valuable and rare art works, book collections, manuscripts, correspondence, and other original material of world-famous artists, musicians, composers, filmmakers, craftsmen, and dramatists.

The Music Division is the custodian of the Library's strongest assemblage of materials in the arts. More than half of the items in some 600 donor-named collections, each ranging in content from a dozen to half a million items, are of European origin. The Library holds 252 music manuscripts by Franz Liszt and many printed scores hand-annotated by Liszt himself. Original manuscripts by Béla Bartók and Zoltán Kodály join autographed scores and correspondence by such composers as Johann Sebastian Bach, Alban Berg, Anton Bruckner, Richard Strauss, Richard Wagner, and Hugo Wolf. The Library's Johannes Brahms holdings are the largest outside Vienna.

Of particular importance is the Albert Schatz Collection of 12,000 German and Italian librettos from the seventeenth and eighteenth centuries, the most complete collection of librettos in the world. The Library owns the original manuscript of Debussy's *Trois Nocturnes*, the 1470 manuscript of Laborde's *Chansonier*, a 1516 edition of *Liber primus missaru* by the Flemish composer Josquin des Prés, and the very rare *Il Primo Libro delli madrigali d' Orlando di Lassus* by the Dutch composer Orlandus Lassus (Rome: Dorico, 1560), of which only one other complete copy is known to exist. Students of music may view holograph scores by Giuseppe Verdi, Nicola Porpora, and Niccolò Paganini (in addition to documents, papers, and other materials in the Paganini collection).

Material on the music of Spain includes musical scores of medieval, Renais-

Franjo Filipović. *Winter.* One of the best examples of South Slav naive art, which is well represented in the collections of the Library of Congress. (From Oto Bihalji-Merin, *Primitive Artists of Yugoslavia,* [Belgrade, 1964], p. 49.) *(General Collections)*

First page of *Two Csárdás, No. 1 Allegro* (s225:1), dated 1884, by the Hungarian composer Franz Liszt. Written in Liszt's own hand, this item is part of the Rosenthal Collection, held by the Music Division of the Library of Congress. *(Music Division)*

sance, and baroque dramas, Catalan songs, "zarzuelas," and works of Manuel de Falla, Isaac Albeniz, and Andrés Segovia.

The Music Division also holds autographed first editions of works by Frédéric Chopin and autographed scores by other Polish composers such as Ignacy Paderewski and Krzysztof Penderecki, among others. The treasures of the Russian music holdings are the archival collections, particularly the Rachmaninoff Archives and the Serge Koussevitzky Music Collection, with numerous original scores, correspondence, notes, diaries, and photographs of major musical personalities throughout the world. The Library also has an impressive set of scores by Czech composers Bedřich Smetana, Antonín Dvořák, and Leoš Janáček, among others. Especially strong is the collection of Czech chamber music, represented by several baroque and early classical figures.

In the Music Division a researcher can find the original recordings of concerts given in the Library of Congress by Gregor Piatigorsky, Artur Rubinstein, the Budapest String Quartet, George Szell, Leopold Stokowski, Claudio Arrau, and others. Musicians can see instruments made by outstanding European artisans, such as the five-string instruments crafted by Antonio Stradivari between 1697 and 1727, the "Brookings" violin made in 1654 by Niccolò Amati, and six-string instruments that are the work of renowned Dutch, French, German, and

Angel on Christ's Tomb, a detail from a fresco in the monastery Mileševa, 1234. The "White Angel," inspiration for later poetry, is a beautiful example of the golden age of old South Slavic church art. (From M. Klarić, *Yugoslavia: A Journey Through Her Art* [Belgrade, 1973], plate xx.) *(General Collections)*

Italian artisans of the seventeenth and eighteenth centuries, donated to the Library by Dr. H. Blaikiston Wilkins. This priceless musical heritage continues to be a focus of interest of many American and European specialists and a valuable source for radio and television programs.

Original scores of contemporary European composers such as Béla Bartók, Henri Dutilleux, Arthur Honneger, Darius Milhaud, Francis Poulenc, Igor Stravinsky, and Iannis Xenakis have been added to the collections through the Library's Serge Koussevitzky Endowment to commission new musical compositions and continue the annual programs where these commissions are performed.

The Gertrude Clarke Whittall Foundation and the Elizabeth Sprague Coolidge Foundation were established in 1934 and 1935, respectively, to support chamber music composition and performance. The Coolidge Collection includes holographs of the more than 300 compositions by eminent twentieth-century composers commissioned by the foundation, as well as Mrs. Coolidge's own compositions and works dedicated to her. The Whittall Collection was begun with the presentation of five Stradivari instruments to the Library of Congress on the condition that they be played at the Library by a quartet in residence. The collection was augmented over the years by original eighteenth-, nineteenth-, and twentieth-century manuscripts, the correspondence of famous European composers, and two

Kazimir Malevich. *Kaiser Wilhelm's Merry-Go-Round* (Moscow, 1915?). Executed in traditional Russian "lubok" or folk style, the poster caricatures the German emperor's early defeats in World War I, quoting him complaining that "I run around and accomplish nothing." (*Russian Poster Collection, Prints and Photographs Division*)

Joseph Daniel von Huber. *Scenographie* (Vienna, 1777). The title sheet of a twenty-four-sheet detailed map of Vienna that was pieced together to make a composite map measuring 350 cm by 410 cm. (*Geography and Map Division*)

special units within the collection: the Niccolò Paganini archive of correspondence, notebooks, musical manuscripts, and posters, many acquired from the Paganini family; and the autographed letters and printed music of Felix Mendelssohn.

After music, the next largest volume of material in the arts is the collection of books on the performing arts—on theater, dance, film, and folk arts—where, again, the European influence is pronounced. Here one discovers remarkable holdings. The George Fabyan collection on the controversy over the authorship of Shakespeare's plays includes thirty-three original works by Sir Francis Bacon published between 1597 and 1640, and the Francis Longe collection of theater works published in England between 1607 and 1812 consists of plays, theatrical adaptations, and translations of over six hundred playwrights. The collection on the performing arts is located in the Library's special reading room in the John F. Kennedy Center for the Performing Arts.

The Lessing J. Rosenwald Collection of 2,600 rare books from the fifteenth through the twentieth centuries, described more fully in the Rare Books and Manuscripts section below, contains books illustrated by Bonnard, Braque, Chagall, Derain, Dufy, Picasso, Rouault, Toulouse-Lautrec, and Utrillo.

For the study of achievements in the plastic arts, the Library has a rich collection of art catalogs from the most important national, international, and individual exhibitions of prominent artists from almost every European country, as well as prints and posters with unique artistic, historic, and scientific value. Of particular interest are the drawings in the Alfred Marie Collection of French renaissance and baroque architecture relating especially to Versailles and other French imperial building projects. The French Political Cartoon Collection encompasses over 200 prints produced between 1789 and 1830 devoted to the French Revolution and the reign of Napoleon Bonaparte. Students of European architecture can find remarkable illustrated volumes, such as the *Life of Thomas Telford, Civil Engineer* and Peter Henry Emerson's *Life and Landscape on the Norfolk Broads* (published in only 200 copies, with forty platinotypes), as well as rich collections of prints of Austrian baroque buildings and Balkan architecture showing strong Eastern and Byzantine influences. In the folio collection, *Villas, Maisons de Ville et de Campagne* by L. Isabey and E. Leblan contains fifty-five chromolithographed plates of the best examples of the heavily ornate style of mid-nineteenth-century France.

Important documents on the history of cinematography and its European heritage are to be found in the collection of the pioneering French filmmaker Georges Méliès. Among the 12,550 films from twenty-three countries held by the Library of Congress, there are approximately fifty early works from France by

The Great MONSTER, REPUBLICAN, *having traversed great part of EUROPE and "shed his blessings all around," animated by a desire to Enlighten all mankind, designs even to grant those Blessings to a Nation of Pirates. — But see BRITANIA has roused her LION to give this Monster, a PROPER RECEPTION.*

Goumont, Pathé, and Cines. The Library's German film collection contains 4,000 feature films, newsreels, and shorts from the Weimar and Third Reich periods alone, among other works. The Italian collection has five hundred documentaries, newsreels, and feature films produced between 1930 and 1943, as well as more contemporary examples of Italian cinematography. Recently the Library has acquired a comprehensive collection of prerevolutionary Russian silent films to add to the existing collection of early Soviet films. Eastern Europe is also represented by filmmakers such as Emir Kosturica, Dušan Makavejev, and Alexander Korda.

W. Brown. *The Great Monster, Republican . . .* (April 1798). Initial British support of the French Revolution waned with the onset of the Terror. By 1798 republicanism was depicted as a monster. *(Popular and Applied Graphic Arts Collection, Prints and Photographs Division)*

Science and Technology

The Library of Congress has assembled one of the world's largest and most diverse collections of scientific and technological literature and one that reflects Europe's centuries-old leadership role in many areas of science. Of the Library's four million scientific monographs amassed, most are written in English and other major European languages; between one-third and one-half are of European provenance. By and large, they are housed in the general collections. All fields are richly represented, excepting clinical medicine and technical agriculture, works of which are collected by the National Library of Medicine and the National Agricultural Library, respectively.

The Library has in its possession many of the early seminal European works pertaining to science. The Rare Book and Special Collections Division holds an original copy of Sir Francis Bacon's *Instauratio Magna*, popularly known as *Novum organum* (London, 1620), which proved persuasive in its explanation of the scientific method. Students of the history of science will be interested in the Library's complete first edition of the works of the Greek mathematician Archimedes, published in 1544 under the Latin title *Opera, quae quidem extant, omnia*. It is this publication that allowed Archimedes's largely forgotten essays, composed in the third century B.C., to leap across the centuries and inspire the mathematical pursuits of Galileo, Descartes, and Newton. In turn, many of the original publications of these three scientists are also available at the Library.

The literature of scientific societies is well represented, beginning with the earliest published records of the late seventeenth century—from the short-lived Accademia del Cimento in Italy, the Royal Society of London, Louis XIV's Académie des Sciences in France, and the Akademie der Wissenschaften in Berlin. The Library possesses impressive holdings from later societies and academies and actively seeks current materials from a large array of European institutions.

With the accelerated pace of information exchange, the research demand for periodical literature in the sciences has greatly outdistanced the demand for monographic works. Perhaps a third of the Library's collection of 61,000 scientific journals is from Europe. Thanks to the Smithsonian deposits from 1866 through 1941, the Library has extensive scientific serial publications from Europe for the nineteenth and first half of the twentieth century. The Library provides strong coverage up to the present of these and other types of scientific periodical literature, including conference proceedings. To aid the researcher in locating such frequently requested materials, numerous bibliographies, indexes, abstracts, and CD-ROM data bases can be found, particularly in the Science and Technology Reading Room.

Petrus Apianus. *Astronomicum caesareum* (Ingolstadt, 1540). One of the colorful astronomical charts called "volvelles," containing movable plates, which are actually working astronomical instruments still able to give accurate measurements. (*Lessing J. Rosenwald Collection, Rare Book and Special Collections Division*)

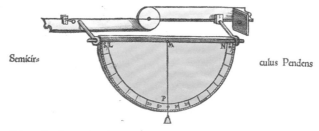

Semicir   culus Pendens

Et hæc quidem de compofitione Torqueti dicta fufficiant, nunc adgrediamur qua nam via proxime
vfum illius tradamus, pati tum facilitate tum breuitate, qua hactenus compofitionem docuimus.

HAEC EST FORMA VIVAQVE TOR:
QVETI MAGO SVIS, ET NVMERIS, ET CIRCV:
lis, & lineamentis, & proportionibus veris perfectiffimè exhibita.

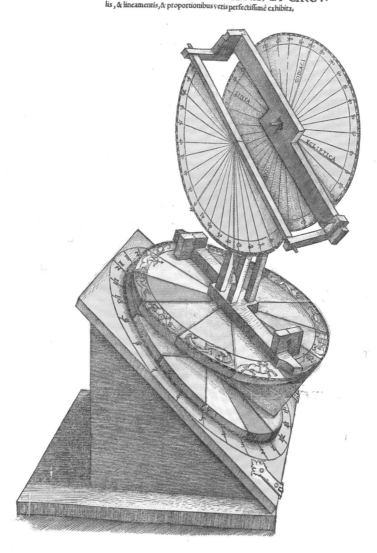

Jefferson's collection contained nearly 400 works from Europe devoted to natural philosophy, agriculture, chemistry, zoology, and the technical arts. It is evident from his correspondence that Jefferson examined these volumes closely. Among the extant works from his library is one by the French chemist Antoine Lavoisier, published in Paris in the revolutionary year of 1789 and entitled *Traité élémentaire de chimie, présenté dans un ordre nouveau et d'après les découvertes modernes; avec figures.* In a letter to a cousin of James Madison, Jefferson took issue with Lavoisier's new terminology, but nonetheless found chemistry "among the most useful of sciences, and big with future discoveries for the utility & safety of the human race."

The Library's holdings of materials relating to the hard sciences such as chemistry, physics, and astronomy are exceptionally strong, with several East European serial holdings unique in North America. An early holding in astronomy is the *Tabulae astronomicae . . .* of the Spanish king Alfonso the Wise, published in Venice in 1483. The most significant early work on the celestial bodies is arguably Nicolaus Copernicus's *De revolutionibus orbium coelestium,* Book 6, which rejected the earth-centered Ptolemaic concept. The Library possesses an original edition from 1543.

European materials in the life sciences of botany, biology, and zoology are well represented in the collections of the Library of Congress, especially in the areas of genetics, microbiology, natural history, ecology, and animal behavior. The Library's psychology collections are quite strong, and include the papers of Sigmund Freud, discussed later. Also impressive are medical holdings from the nineteenth and first half of the twentieth century, before the National Library of Medicine assumed major responsibility for acquisitions in clinical medicine in the early 1950s. Likewise, agricultural literature is well represented until that time, when the Library of Congress deferred acquisition of technical agriculture and veterinary medicine to the National Agricultural Library.

The Library's efforts to acquire European materials pertaining to the earth sciences extend as far back as the purchase of Jefferson's library in 1815. The current European collections in this realm are quite strong, especially in mineralogy, stratigraphy, and other geologic fields, but also in such areas as geography, paleontology, biodiversity, environmental pollution, and environmental law. The extensive materials from Western Europe and Russia pertaining to arctic and alpine research form a large contribution to two ongoing bibliographies published by the Library's Science and Technology Division, the *Bibliography on Cold Regions Science and Technology* and the *Antarctic Bibliography.*

The holdings of the Library of Congress in literature pertaining to math-

Frontispiece by Stefano della Bella to Galileo's *Dialogo . . . sopra i due massimi sistemi del mondo tolemaico, e copernicano* (Fiorenza, 1632) shows Aristotle, Ptolemy, and Copernicus discussing matters of astronomy. It was the *Dialogo* and its open defense of Copernican heliocentrism that occasioned Galileo's trial and his abjuration of the work itself. *(Rare Book and Special Collections Division)*

ematics and computer science are impressive, including such fields as numerical analysis, cybernetics, and telecommunications. Particularly noteworthy are the extensive runs of Russian, Polish, and other European serials in these areas. The Russian forte in mathematics is reflected in the Library's extensive holdings of mathematics journals and monographs from that part of the world.

The Library of Congress collections of technological literature are at least as large as those pertaining to science. An early landmark of both theoretical scientific and technological literature was observed with the publication in eighteenth-century France of Denis Diderot's *Encyclopédie ou Dictionnaire raisonné des sciences, des arts, et des métiers.* The Library possesses a complete set of the first edition in seventeen volumes of text and eleven volumes of engravings.

The history and application of many areas of European technology are well represented in the Library's collections, such as electrical engineering, mechanical engineering, machinery, aeronautics, astronautics and photography, and especially chemical technology.

The Technical Reports Section of the Library's Science and Technology Division has amassed nearly four million technical reports, primarily on microfiche. Many of the earlier

Andreas Vesalius. *De humani corporis fabrica,* libri septem (Basileae [Ex Officina I. Oporini, 1543]). This publication of the young professor at Padua revolutionized the science and teaching of anatomy. Vesalius based his work on the dissection of humans rather than of other primates. *(Lessing J. Rosenwald Collection, Rare Book and Special Collections Division)*

European technical reports after World War II pertained to atomic energy; more current reports focus on the environment, commercial applications, and technology transfer. There are regional strengths: the Finns and other Scandinavians, for example, produce technical reports important to construction research, whereas Dutch technical reports are strong in agriculture and the environment. Many European countries provide technical reports on mathematics and on information and computer sciences. Increased efforts are being expended to collect similar "gray" literature (literature not published through regular channels), often published in low press runs by European research institutes.

Similarly, the Library strives to collect technical standards from selected industrialized countries. The Technical Reports Section maintains the only official hard-copy set of Soviet (now Russian) national standards to be found in North America, as well as microfilm copies of national standards for France, Germany, and Great Britain, and the integrated standards for the European Union.

A landmark for the Library came about with the acquisition of a collection of important documents on German industry, known as the FIAT and BIOS reports, acquired from Allied intelligence agencies shortly after World War II. These documents provide a clear picture of the nature of German technological advances prior to and during the war and demonstrate Nazi German industry's total orientation toward armaments production. They encompass a variety of captured German technical documentation, especially technical reports, but also patent applications from 1939 to 1945.

For all subjects, the Library of Congress seeks to acquire translations from foreign languages into English only. To meet the high demand for translations of scientific literature, the Library has collected hundreds of thousands of documents in this area. For example, extensive runs of the Joint Publications Research Service, consisting primarily of translations of technical literature from the former Soviet bloc, and of commercially produced, cover-to-cover translations of Western European and Russian scientific journals are available in the collections.

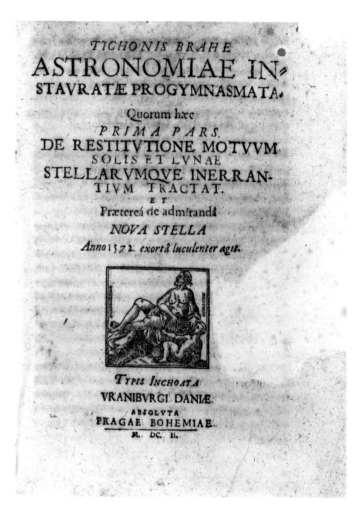

Tycho Brahe. *Astronomiae instauratae progymnasmata* (Prague, 1602), title page. The first of a projected three volumes on recent astronomical phenomena, this volume reproduces Brahe's "De nova stella" of 1572, based on accurate observations and representing the modern scientific method. *(Rare Book and Special Collections Division)*

Special Collections

Special collections pertaining to Europe include personal libraries, illustrated books, collections of unusual provenance, and author, subject, or language collections. Of the hundreds of special collections in the Library of Congress, those that were seminal to large-scale collecting by the Library in a particular field deserve special mention. They include collections that are strictly European and those with a strong European component.

As noted earlier, the broad subject base of Jefferson's collection stamped the Library from the beginning as something more than an assemblage of law books for the use of legislators, although it did remain strictly a library for the use of the Congress for another fifty years. As with the burning of the Capitol in 1814, once again a fire triggered a significant advance in the development of the collections a half-century later. In 1866, the Smithsonian Institution's 40,000 volumes, chiefly in science and technology with a very strong European representation, were deposited at the Library of Congress following a fire at the Smithsonian the previous year, with the provision that "the public shall have access thereto for purposes of consultation." Besides providing a significant new subject dimension to the congressional collection, the Smithsonian deposit initiated the Library's program of exchanges with institutions abroad. At the time of its incorporation into the Library's collections in 1941, the deposit formed a separate collection of more than a half-million volumes, the major part of the Library's European holdings in science and technology. Today collections in science and technology make up 25 percent of the Library's general collections.

Occasionally the acquisition of a special collection marked a quantum leap in the Library's holdings on a single country. Thus the inventory of foreign books in the *Report of the Librarian of Congress for the Fiscal Year Ending June 30, 1901* had given the Russian total as only 569 volumes, exclusive of the Smithsonian deposit. Six years later the purchase of the private collection of the Siberian merchant Gennadii Yudin brought a staggering total of 68,000 volumes of Russian-language materials to the Library. In the words of President Theodore Roosevelt, the Yudin collection "will give the Library of Congress preeminence in this particular field, not only in the United States, but as far as I know in the world generally outside of Russia; and this in a field not yet developed at all in America."

Like the Jefferson collection, the Yudin collection was broad-based and the finest private library in his country. It was a working library, but it also contained more than 4,000 rare items, including long runs of eighteenth-century periodicals that give the researcher an in-depth view of the intellectual movements and activities of the period. Yudin's library created the base upon which the present 700,000-

Children near Belozersk. One of a collection of 2,500 color photographs, taken between 1906 and 1912 by Russian photographer Sergei Prokudin-Gorskii, which give intimate glimpses into the life of late imperial Russia. *(Prokudin-Gorskii Collection, Prints and Photographs Division)*

volume Russian-language collection of the Library of Congress would be built.

In similar fashion, albeit on a considerably smaller scale, a significant addition to the Library's then-modest Bulgarian collection was the purchase in 1949 of the Early Bulgarian Imprint Collection from the bibliophile Todor Plochev. These 650 books represent the best titles published outside Bulgaria during the Bulgarian Renaissance (1806–78), a time when publishing in the Bulgarian language in Bulgaria was forbidden under Ottoman rule. The Library's Bulgarian collection has since grown to approximately 40,000 volumes.

The nucleus of the Library's extensive collection of works on Portuguese history and literature emerged in 1927 and 1929 through the purchase of the Portuguese Manuscript Collection, with items dating from 1438 into the twentieth century, including books, manuscripts, and letters of diplomats. A special connection to South America are the 201 letters to or by Manoel de Cunha Menezes, captain general of Pernambuco and Bahia (1774–79).

The Library's considerable holdings in aeronautics were initiated by the acquisition in 1930 of the Tissandier Collection, relating to the history of aeronautics from 1776 to 1914. The collection was assembled by Albert, Gaston, and Paul Tissandier, balloonists and aeronautical historians, and it contained, according to Librarian of Congress Herbert Putnam (tenure 1899–1939), "approximately all the worth-while aeronautics literature published in France up to 1900." This acquisition accompanied the creation in the Library of a Division of Aeronautics in 1930 and an aggressive acquisitions program that brought gifts from individuals and organizations prominent in American aeronautics.

In a totally different vein, magic, illusion, spiritualism, and magical apparatus—much of it with a European flavor—are represented in two special collections. Books numbering nearly 4,000 volumes as well as prints, playbills, pamphlets, scrapbooks, and periodicals on magic, witchcraft, demonology, psychic phenomena, and spiritualism formed the bequest of Harry Houdini, the son of a Budapest rabbi, who became a world-renowned magician. The Library received this collection in 1927, a year after Houdini's death. Houdini's bequest was followed by the 10,000-item collection of publications and pictorial material relating to magic and magical apparatus presented to the Library in 1955 by John J. and Hanna M. McManus and Morris N. and Chesley V. Young. This collection contains works, inter alia, on conjuring, ventriloquism, fortune-telling, spiritualism, witchcraft, hypnotism, mind reading, and explanations of magicians' tricks.

The Library's special collections are not confined to written matter. The Archive of Hispanic Literature on Tape comprises recordings of prominent au-

Theuerdank (Augsburg, 1517), illustration no. 60. This work, which presents a loosely disguised portrait of Emperor Maximillian I, was the first to use Fraktur before it became the standard German letterform. Included are many scenes of everyday life in the sixteenth century. *(Lessing J. Rosenwald Collection, Rare Book and Special Collections Division)*

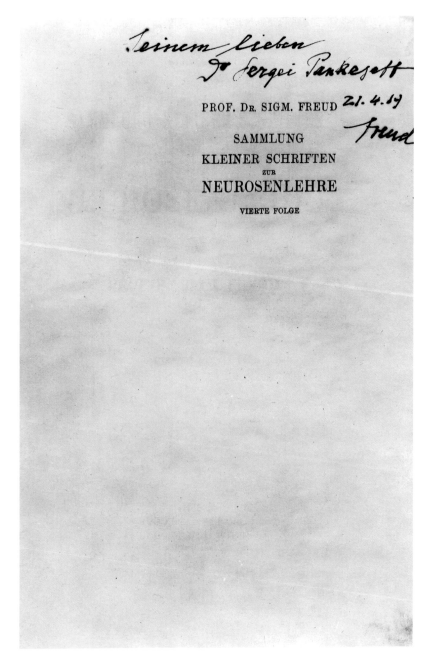

thors of Spanish and Portuguese works in Europe and America. The archive was begun in 1942 and now consists of more than 600 readings of writers that include seven Nobel prize winners, three of them from Spain. A similar program, the Archive of World Literature on Tape, was begun in 1977 to include those countries and languages not represented by the Archive of Hispanic Literature on Tape. For the next dozen years this program proved especially valuable for recording authors from the communist countries of Europe who, although they hesitated to record for the American audience in their own countries, felt at ease recording at the Library of Congress. Recordings of authors from the European democracies are also represented in this collection.

The special-format collections also include glass-plate negatives in the Prokudin-Gorskii and Detroit Publishing Company collections. Sergei Mikhailovich Prokudin-Gorskii, Russian pioneer in color photography and "photographer to the tsar," photographed artworks, architecture, industry, topography, individuals, and daily life in both European and Asiatic Russia, mostly between 1909 and 1911. The Library of Congress purchased this collection of 1,900 negatives in 1948. Contact prints, made from the negatives and mounted in fifteen albums, are available for examination by the reader. The Detroit Publishing Company Collections of 18,500 glass negatives and 22,000 photoprints depict historic sites, natural landmarks, industry, sports activities, and buildings in America and in Europe in the period 1898–1924. There is strong representation of Austria-Hungary, Russia, and the Balkans, as well as more conventional scenes of Western and Southern Europe.

The Otto Vollbehr collection of more than 3,000 fifteenth-century incunabula and early printed books acquired by an act of Congress in 1930 taken together with the Lessing J. Rosenwald gift to the Library of Congress (1943–75) of more than 2,600 illustrated books from the fifteenth to the twentieth centuries, and the Wilhelm Schreiber collection (1929) of more than 20,000 book illustrations dating from the fifteenth through the eighteenth centuries make the Library of Congress a major source of research on the history of European printing and the book arts.

Collections pertaining to political events include the German Captured Documents collection, which consists of 350,000 documents from the interwar and World War II period, including records of the treatment of the territories occupied by German forces during the war. A particular interest of Librarian of Congress James H. Billington (Librarian since 1987), the Soviet Independent Press collection amounts to some 20,000 issues of 3,000 serial titles, representing every political shade and faction from monarchist to extreme left, published during the period of exuberance between the promulgation of more liberal press laws and the demise of the Soviet Union at the end of 1991.

Notable collections devoted to individual European personalities include, for example, 500 volumes assembled by the Law Library of the writings and various editions of the great English jurist William Blackstone, whose *Commentaries on the Laws of England* was the first systematic treatise on the principles and decisions of English common law. Similarly, beginning in the 1950s the Library began to form an important collection of the papers and early editions of the works of Sigmund Freud, the founder of psychoanalysis. In addition to an extensive collection of Freud's manuscripts and correspondence—among them, the manuscripts of the case of Sergius Pankejeff, the "Wolfman"—the Library holds a number of presentation copies from Freud's library. Today the collection amounts to some 80,000 manuscript pieces and several hundred books. A third such collection on an individual personality came to the Library when Danish actor Jean Hersholt and Mrs. Hersholt donated their comprehensive collection of works by and about the author Hans Christian Andersen. The gift, which included first editions, manuscripts, letters, presentation copies, and pictorial material as well as translations, constitutes the most outstanding Andersen collection outside Denmark.

Sigmund Freud. *Sammlung kleiner Schriften zur Neurosenlehre* (Leipzig, Vienna, 1906). In 1919, Freud signed and presented this 1906 edition to Sergius Pankejeff, the "Wolfman." *(Freud Collection, Rare Book and Special Collections Division)*

Rare Books and Manuscripts

Both the original congressional library, organized to meet the practical demands of the legislators for law and general literature, and Jefferson's library, which expanded considerably the subject and language scope of the collections, held primarily modern, scholarly editions. Until the middle of the nineteenth century, it was in a somewhat serendipitous manner that the Library acquired a number of rare books and manuscripts. Not until the second half of the nineteenth century, in the expansionist and nationalist spirit of the time, were the Library's legislative and national functions permanently linked. Librarian of Congress Ainsworth Rand Spofford (tenure 1864–97), while continuing to develop the legislative library for the Congress, actively began to build a national collection for the American people that included both rare book and manuscript collections, some of European provenance. Spofford began to cull rare books from the Library's collections and to designate them for a special collection in his "Office," a designation still found on many bibliographical records.

In 1897, when the Library moved out of the Capitol into its own building, now named the Thomas Jefferson Building, one of the new departments created was the Manuscript Division. In the magnificent new building, European in style and in orientation, European rare books and manuscripts henceforth figured prominently in the collections. A history of remarkable acquisitions involving many generous donors has created at the Library of Congress one of the stronger collections of European rare books in North America and important collections of manuscripts and other rarities that are European either in origin or in focus.

European rarities, in book and other print formats and in manuscript, are held both in specific collections and in more general collections throughout the Library. Overall, they support a full chronological, geographical, and subject range of studies. First, early, or other rare editions of milestones in classical and European thought are basic to the Library's European holdings of rare books. Thus, the Library holds rare editions of writers such as Herodotus, Lucretius, Augustine, Andreas Vesalius, Nicolaus Copernicus, Ignatius of Loyola, Francesco Guicciardini, Giorgio Vasari, Tycho Brahe, René Descartes, William Harvey, Jacques-Bénigne Bossuet, Giambattista Vico, Linnaeus, Montesquieu, Edward Gibbon, Immanuel Kant, Mikhail Lomonosov, Edmund Burke, Mary Wollstonecraft, John Keats, Fyodor Dostoyevsky, Jacob Burckhardt, Johann Wolfgang von Goethe, Taras Shevchenko, Sarah Bernhardt, Marie Curie, Sigmund Freud, Thomas Mann, Ortega y Gasset, and Vladimir Nabokov.

In 1926 the Library published a desiderata list of what Librarian of Congress Herbert Putnam termed "bibliographical monumenta, which should indisputably

Grand Coutumier de Normandie (1480). An illustration of early customary law, this miniature depicts a bailiff and several knights visiting a sickroom, probably to verify that the defendant is too ill to appear in court. *(Law Library, Rare Book Room)*

ᵴ enſuit la quarte
diſtinction de ce liure.
en la quelle len trai
te de delayemens cõ

be represented in the National Library of the United States." Putnam felt that Americans should be able to turn to the Library of Congress as an ultimate resource in the same way that Britons were able to turn to what was then called the British Museum Library (now the British Library). This list, which includes American, European, and Hebrew-language titles, has served as a major collection focus of rare European works. Over the years through gifts and purchases the Library has been able to acquire many of them.

Among the Library's rare book and manuscript strengths and acquisition focuses are subjects such as European law, European music, the history of science and technology, historiography, travel literature, the Reformation, European exploration and settlement, European documentation related to American history, gastronomy, magic and spiritualism, the French Revolution, Russian history and literature, Freud, the Third Reich, and diplomatic relations between the United States and the countries of Europe.

Early legal material provides valuable resources for the study of European cultural and social history and documents early European government and the origin of legal codes that later extended well beyond Europe. The Library holds major collections of Roman law, canon law, and consilia and the largest collection outside France of French *coutumes*—local customary laws. Treasures include a thirteenth-century vellum manuscript of Justinian's *Institutes cum glossa Francisci Accursii;* the beautifully illustrated *Grand Coutumier de Normandie;* a ca. 1500 manuscript of the *Sachsenspiegel,* the oldest German law code, compiled between 1220 and 1235; a first edition of *De Jure Belli ac Pacis* by Hugo Grotius, published in 1625; and rare printed editions of the *Russkaia Pravda,* the oldest East European code, compiled in the eleventh and twelfth centuries.

The John Boyd Thacher collection of manuscripts includes European autographs from as early as the fourteenth century, including European monarchs such as Charles V of France, Elizabeth I of England, and Frederick the Great of Prussia. The early documentation of European cooking begins with the Library's mid-fifteenth-century Italian manuscript "Libro de arte coquinaria" of Maestro Martino and is also well illustrated by the Dutch wood-block book *Hier beginnt eenen nyeuwen coock boeck . . . y Gerardus Vorselman* (Antwerp, 1560).

The Library's collection of incunabula—the largest in the Western Hemisphere—includes examples from approximately two-thirds of about 1,080 known European presses of the fifteenth century, in-depth representations of every aspect of fifteenth-century printing, and books of outstanding importance in extraordinary condition. Here we can only skim the surface of the remarkable riches

Dutch Bible (Amsterdam, 1702). This Bible, the first to include a map, has over 160 hand-colored illustrations by Romeyn de Hooghe, perhaps the most significant Dutch book illustrator of the late seventeenth and early eighteenth centuries. Folio no. 149 shows Daniel in the lion's den. (*Rare Book and Special Collections Division*)

Rom. de ..Hooge Inventor et fecit   J. Lamsvelt excudit cum Privil.

DICHTKUNDIGE VERKLAARING van de LXXXII. AFBEELDING.

Hier word de bitsche Nyd met 's Konings wrok betaalt,   't Verschynsel van een Ram, die 't woeft gedierte velt,
Daar Daniel van 't Hof en d'Afgunst zegepraalt,   Verslagen door een Bok; en d'Engel die voorspelt
En ziet zyn vyanden verscheurt door wilde Leeuwen.   Den stryd van Michaël tot heil der laater' Eeuwen.

Ostrih Bible (1581), title page. One of the greatest monuments of sixteenth-century Ukrainian culture, this Bible has become the common heritage of all Christian East Slavs. (*Rare Book and Special Collections Division*)

A Boare, a Mastiff, a Thistle, an engraving by Wenceslaus Hollar, a seventeenth-century Czech artist who emigrated from Bohemia, lived in Frankfurt, Strasbourg, Cologne, and London, and achieved an international reputation as a copperengraver and miniature painter. *(Prints and Photographs Division)*

of the Library's treasures from this era. They include one of the three known complete copies of the Gutenberg Bible printed on vellum (1454–55), the first European book printed from movable type, found in the Vollbehr Collection; Guillelmus Duranti's *Rationale divinorum officiorum* ([Mainz]: Johann Fust and Peter Schoeffer, 6 October 1459) in the Thacher Collection; and Fust and Schoeffer's 1462 Latin Bible (Mainz: Johann Fust and Peter Schoeffer, 14 August 1462) in the Rosenwald Collection. The 1488 Paris edition of Olivier de La Marche's *Le Chevalier délibéré,* considered the finest illustrated French book of the fifteenth century (Paris: [Guy Marchand or Antoine Caillaut] for Antoine Vérard, 8 August 1488) is found in the Rosenwald Collection as well, as are Dante's *La Commedia* with copper engravings ascribed to Baccio Baldini (Florence: Nicolaus Laurentii, Alamanus, 30 August 1481) and the chess game *De ludo scachorum* ([Bruges: William Caxton, after 31 March, 1474]).

In 1993, the Library acquired another extremely rare example of fifteenth-century printing, a pamphlet commissioned by King John II of Portugal and presented by the leading Latinist of the Portuguese court, Vasco Fernandes— *Velasci Ferdinandi vtriusique iuris consulti illustrissimi regis Portugallie oratoris ad Innocentium.viii. pontificem maximum de obedientia Oratio* [Rome: Stephen Plannck, 1488–90]. The first printed account of the Portuguese discoveries, it is an obedience oration presented to the new pope, Innocent VIII, that announces to the pontiff the inauguration of the European age of discovery. The Library's 100 million first item, the priceless pamphlet was acquired through a gift from John E. Velde, Jr.

European religious life and art are heavily documented areas with books and manuscripts such as French books of hours; the exquisite Nekcsei-Lipócz Bible—a Latin Bible probably written and decorated in Hungary, ca. 1335–40; the Gutenberg Bible; the Giant Bible of Mainz; and many European vernacular Bibles, including the oldest Croatian book, the *Missale Glagoliticum* (Venice, 1483), the Czech Kutná Hora Bible (1489); the *Complutensian Polyglot Bible* (6 vols. [Alcala, 1514–17]); and Ivan Fedorov's complete Church Slavic Ostrih (Ostrog) Bible of 1581. Also in the collection are early works by Martin Luther and the rare 1651 edition of Patriarch Nikon's *Kormchaia kniga,* a compilation of Orthodox doctrines and practices which was instrumental in creating the Old Believer schism in the Russian Orthodox Church.

Rare collections of European literature and history focused on individual cultures defined by language include the Accademia della Crusca Collection, containing Italian publications ranging from the sixteenth to the nineteenth centuries, the sources from which this academy wrote its authoritative dictionary of the

William Blake. *Songs of innocence and experience, showing the two contrary states of the human soul* (London, 1794). This "illuminated book" was published in 1794 and hand-colored by Blake in 1826. The image of "The Blossom" is a prime example of Blake's brilliant use of color. *(Lessing J. Rosenwald Collection, Rare Book and Special Collections Division)*

The Blossom.

Merry Merry Sparrow
Under leaves so green
A happy Blossom
Sees you swift as arrow
Seek your cradle narrow
Near my Bosom.

Pretty Pretty Robin
Under leaves so green
A happy Blossom
Hears you sobbing sobbing
Pretty Pretty Robin
Near my Bosom.

Italian language; the Raymond Toinet Collection, especially strong in seventeenth-century French literature; and the Francis Longe Collection of theatrical works printed in English from 1607 to 1812. Rare books by Goethe, Schiller, and Lessing, as well as an early verse translation by Johann Gustav Büschung (1815) of the Middle High German Epic *Das Lied der Nibelungen,* and the first edition of Goethe's *Stella, Ein Schauspiel für Liebende in fünf Akten* (1776) are found in the Deneke Collection. The Portuguese Manuscript Collection includes materials from 1438 to the early twentieth century relating to various aspects of Portuguese history, society, literature, religion, and culture. Several collections focus on individual European writers. One of the world's major Cervantes collections, given to the Library by Leonard Kebler, illustrates Spain's golden age and includes treasures such as the second state of the first edition of Don Quixote (Madrid: Juan de la Cuesta, 1605), identified only in this century. The George Fabyan collection, focused on cryptography, includes valuable material related to the Shakespeare-Bacon controversy. The Library's extensive collection on Rudyard Kipling, the result of several donors' bequests, includes rarities such as the earliest known draft of "Mowgli's Brothers," the first story in *The Jungle Book.* William Blake, Jules Verne, and Hugh Walpole are the focus of several collections. The Library also holds manuscripts of work by Shelley, Wilde, Shaw, and Ibsen.

European travel, exploration, and expansion are documented in rarities such as the *De consuetudinibus et conditionibus orientalium regionum* (Antwerp, 1483–85), a version of Marco Polo's exploits, and Bernhard Breidenbach's account of his pilgrimage to the Holy Land, *Peregrinatio* (Mainz, 1486). Missionary accounts dating from the sixteenth century to texts such as Pehr Högström's *Beskrifning offwer de til Sweriges Krona lydande Lapmarker* (Stockholm, 1747) and David Livingstone's *Missionary Travels and Researches in South Africa* (London, 1857) are important for the study of European exploration. The Library's varied holdings on European involvement in the Americas is discussed below in the European Americana section.

The Czech statesman Thomas G. Masaryk's complete original handwritten copy of his book *Nová Evropa* (The New Europe), the final version of which was completed during his stay in Washington in 1918, is an example of important facets of the history of twentieth-century Europe that are documented by several fascinating items and collections. The manuscript was donated by Masaryk's former private secretary Dr. Jaroslav Císař.

A remarkable story unfolded shortly after World War II when an American soldier saved from destruction a miscellany of books, albums, and printed materials from the Reichskanzlei Library in Berlin. Another American rescued the pri-

Paul Fargue. *D'après Paris.* (Paris, 1931). Paul Bonet's binding is a striking example of art deco design. (*Lessing J. Rosenwald Collection, Rare Book and Special Collections Division*)

vate book collections of several high-ranking Nazi party officials, including Hitler, Göring, and Himmler, and had the materials shipped to Washington, where, with the Reichskanzlei materials, they now make up the Third Reich Collection of the Library of Congress.

Another gripping tale from the Second World War details the background of the 1946 publication of the Ciano diaries, smuggled out of Italy after Mussolini had executed his son-in-law former statesman Galeazzo Ciano. The story is recounted in the working papers—the Galeazzo Ciano Papers—donated in 1955 by their publisher, Doubleday and Company, Inc.

No less significant was the Library's acquisition of the papers of journalists, writers, and literary editors Janet Flanner and Solita Solano as gifts from the authors over a ten-year period (1967–77). For half a century (1925–75) Flanner wrote the column "Letter from Paris" for *The New Yorker* magazine. Much of the Flanner-Solano Collection relates to the literary and intellectual society and life of Paris and includes writings by and correspondence or photographs of individuals such as Aragon, Karen Blixen, Colette, Gurdjieff, Malraux, Olga Petrova, Dame Edith Sitwell, and Thornton Wilder.

The Lessing J. Rosenwald Collection, the greatest overall gift of rare books to the Library of Congress, focuses on the Western illustrated book from the fifteenth through the twentieth century. Rosenwald once remarked that "an interest in books naturally leads to an interest in the development of printing." His collection includes significant holdings of Western European type specimens, decrees governing printing and bookselling, and printing manuals from France, England, Italy, and Germany. Among its particular strengths are early wood-block books such as *Apocalypsis sancti Johannis* (Germany, ca. 1470) and the *Nuremberg Chronicle* (1493), the most heavily illustrated book from the late fifteenth century. Also noteworthy are neoclassical eighteenth-century French illustrated books. For example, the 1751 French edition of Erasmus's *L'Eloge de la folie* illustrated by Charles Eisen includes seventeen original drawings by the illustrator bound in. The drawings by Gravelot for Boccaccio's *Decamerone*, published in 1757, are also part of the collection.

Another highlight of the Lessing J. Rosenwald Collection is the *livre d'artiste*, a genre which was developed in France during the first quarter of the twentieth century and then spread throughout Europe, offering examples of modern illustration, typography, and binding. Here one comes across works by Bonnard, Braque, Chagall, Clair, Cocteau, Derain, Duchamp, Dufy, Matisse, Picasso, Rouault, Toulouse-Lautrec, Utrillo, and de Vlaminck.

Henri Matisse. *Jazz* ([Paris] 1947). The only publication of which Matisse was both author and illustrator, *Jazz* embodies the tradition of the artist's book. *(Lessing J. Rosenwald Collection, Rare Book and Special Collections Division)*

Maps

The Library of Congress possesses more than one million items of European cartographic material, including maps, atlases, globes, microforms, and aerial and remote sensing maps, as well as reference books and pamphlets. The collection encompasses all countries and regions of Europe at various scales on various media, ranging from hand-written navigational charts from the fourteenth century to photographs taken from orbiting satellites in the twentieth.

Starting with the fifteenth century, the collection faithfully reflects important trends in the history of European cartography. At that time the first of a string of events and innovations occurred that would spur European interest in geography and mapmaking. In 1453, the Ottoman Turks captured Constantinople, capital of the millennium-old Byzantine Empire, and the resulting flood of Greek refugee-scholars into Italy was accompanied by an influx of ancient manuscripts, including the *Geōgraphikē hyphēgēsis* (Guide to Geography) of Claudius Ptolemaeus (Ptolemy). Two years later Johann Gutenberg introduced movable-type printing into Europe, and later in the century the introduction of engraved copper plates for printing maps allowed more detail to be published than previously attainable with woodcuts. Concurrent with these technological innovations were the beginnings of European exploration of the non-European world and the general Renaissance interest in science and learning. One result of these events was the birth and rapid development of map publishing in Europe, beginning in Italy in the 1470s.

It is fitting that Ptolemy's *Geōgraphikē* was the first cartographic work to be published. Written in Alexandria, Egypt, in the second century after Christ, it appeared in at least thirty-one published editions in various parts of Europe between 1475 and 1600. The Library of Congress possesses many of these editions, including the first, published in Venice in 1475, which contains no maps. It also holds the subsequent Rome 1478 edition, which contains maps of the world as then known, in black and white, and the Ulm 1482 edition, the first edition to be published outside of Italy and to possess maps in color. Later editions display cartographic innovations and incorporate new maps. For example, the 1513 edition, published in Strasbourg, represents the earliest example of map printing in three colors, and the 1545 Münster edition contains the first map of Bohemia drawn by a Czech. The Library of Congress also possesses many facsimile editions of the *Geōgraphikē* published in the twentieth century.

As map-making techniques moved northward from Italy, so did the production of maps and atlases. The Library's collection contains examples of the work of all the great Dutch publishing houses from the sixteenth through eighteenth

Battista Agnese. *Portolan Atlas* (Venice, 1544). Hand-drawn and painted on vellum, the ten double-page maps of this atlas were prepared for the abbot of St. Vaast at Arras. Map no. 8 shows Europe in the sixteenth century. *(Geography and Map Division)*

Jodocus Hondius. *Nova Europae Descriptio.* Copper engraving, 37 by 50 cm. From Gerardi Mercatoris, *Atlas sive cosmographicae meditationes de fabrica mundi et fabricati figura* (Amsterdam, 1619) [between pages 33 and 34]. This map of Europe first appeared as one of thirty-seven new maps in Jodocus Hondius's original issuance of Mercator's landmark work published in Amsterdam in 1606. This illustration is reproduced from the Library of Congress 1619 edition of Mercator's atlas. A publisher and printer, as well as an engraver, a stamp-cutter, and a map- and globe-maker, Hondius, and later his heirs, continued and enhanced the tradition of the great Dutch cartographers. *(Geography and Map Division)*

centuries, including a collection of various editions of Abraham Ortelius's *Theatrum orbis terrarum*, first published in Antwerp in 1570. Unlike previous editors of published map collections, Ortelius standardized the format of the maps he published, and he also used the work of only one cartographer for a given country. His first edition contains the oldest map of Hungary, compiled by a certain Lázár, a secretary to the prince primate of the Roman Catholic Church in Hungary. A 1573 edition contains the first independent map of Moravia by Fabricius, and a 1579 edition includes maps of Slovakia by Lazius and Sambucus. Another notable cartographer from this time whose works are well represented in the Library is the great Flemish geographer Gerardus Mercator. The Library possesses the first edition of his *Atlas sive cosmographicae meditationes de fabrica mundi et fabricati figura* (Duisburg, 1595), the first uniform collection of maps to bear the title *Atlas*.

Other notable items dating from the sixteenth century include materials from the Sir Francis Drake Collection, among them Nicola van Sype's engraved map of the Elizabethan explorer's route around the globe and a letter exchanged between the master cartographers Mercator and Ortelius. The Melville Eastham Collection, also worthy of note, consists of sixteenth- and seventeenth-century atlases and printed maps, including those issued by the important cartographers and atlas publishers of that period. Approximately half of the maps depict regions in England, France, and Germany.

The Library's collection of seventeenth-century European cartography includes a number of fine collections of atlases printed in Rome, Bologna, and Venice. Noteworthy are the globes crafted by Vincenzo Coronelli, along with other rare late seventeenth-century Venetian globes. Coronelli's *Libro de' globi*, published in Venice in the 1690s, catalogs all the globes he produced. From the same period in northern Europe, the Library of Congress owns many of the globes, sea charts, wall maps, and atlases created by the Dutch publishers Willem Jansz Blaeu and his sons Cornelius and Joan. The Blaeu *Atlas maior* with text in Latin

Frederik de Wit. *Theatrum iconographicum omnium urbium* (Amsterdam, 1700). This late seventeenth-century aerial perspective view of Maastricht is in an atlas collection of plans of cities in the Netherlands. *(Geography and Map Division)*

(11 volumes), Dutch (9 volumes), German (9 volumes), French (12 volumes), and Spanish (10 volumes), all bound in contemporary vellum or velvet, are to be found at the Library. Of special importance to one of post-Soviet Eastern Europe's newly independent countries is the first individually published map to use the term "Ukraina" in its title: *Delineatio generalis Camporum Desertorum vulgo Ukraina: cum adjacentibus provinciis . . .* (Gedanum: Beauplan, 1648). A superb example of the engraving art of Willem Hondius of Gdańsk, the plate was sold to the Polish crown in 1652.

Several of the Library's priceless maps of the New World drawn by European explorers are described in the European Americana section below, as are three important British collections related to the American Revolution.

The Library's holdings of eighteenth-century maps reflect the preeminence of France in the development of scientific cartography during that era. The transition from speculative cartography to maps based on precise surveying and the corresponding decline in artistic embellishment can be observed in the collection of maps by Alexis Hubert Jaillot, Guillaume De Lisle, and the two Robert de Vaugondys. Especially numerous in the collections are multisheet French topographical maps from the late eighteenth and early nineteenth centuries, such as the 180-sheet Cassini survey of France (1789), represented in the collection by a hand-colored, uncreased copy. The late eighteenth century is also represented in part of the Hauslab-Liechtenstein Collection, acquired in 1975, which features 3,600 maps of Central Europe, Russia, and the Middle East by the Austrian military cartographer Franz Ritter von Hauslab.

Students of cartography will find the Library's nineteenth-century holdings as impressive as those of earlier periods. An extensive collection of Portuguese colonial maps makes the Library of Congress one of the largest centers for research on those far-flung domains. Outstanding examples include Armando Cortesão's six-volume *Portugaliae monumenta cartographica* and many maps published by the Agencia Geral do Ultramar, such as the *Carta da Colônia da Guiné Portuguesa* (1889), the *Carta da Africa meridional portuguesa* (1886), and the *Carta de Angola, contendo indicações de produção e salubridade* (1885).

Another collection of great value and interest is a series published by the Military-Geographic Institute in Vienna for the whole Austro-Hungarian Empire, at scales of 1:75,000 (1875–) and later 1:25,000 (1900–). These maps reveal villages, physical features, and other details not visible on maps with larger scales. At the same time, they provide the Hungarian and German place-names for towns and cities that are now located in the Czech Republic, Slovakia, Ukraine, Croatia, Ser-

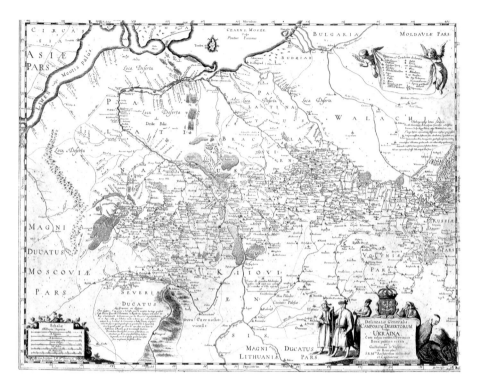

Capt. Guillaume le Vasseur de Beauplan. *Delineatio generalis camporum desertorum vulgo Ukraina cum adjacentibus provinciis* (Gdańsk [Danzig]: Willem Hondius, 1648). Commissioned by the Polish crown, this is the first scientifically measured map of Ukraine and adjacent lands and is unusual in its perspective, showing south at the top of the map. *(Geography and Map Division)*

bia, and Romania and, hence, are especially valuable for historians and genealogists.

Size and comprehensiveness alone would distinguish the Library's collection of twentieth-century cartography relating to Europe, but its rare items deserve special mention. The 278,000-item Woodrow Wilson Papers include many maps—often modified by hand—brought to the peace conferences following the First World War, including a pen-and-ink watercolor map of the proposed boundaries of Poland with the annotation in the lower margin: "Washington, October 8, 1918." Also dating from World War I is the John L. Hines Collection, which contains printed maps bearing annotations on troop placement and battery positions relating to Hines's activities on the French and Belgian fronts.

Not to be overlooked is the Library's comprehensive collection of topographic, geological, and topical maps from Russia and the former Soviet Union. Most of these maps were issued by the Soviet cartographic agency, although a substantial number of prerevolutionary maps of Russia were acquired with the purchase of the Yudin collection in 1906.

European Americana and American Europeana

Webster's New World Dictionary defines Americana as "books, papers, objects, facts, etc. having to do with America, its people, and its history." By that general definition, Americana probably accounts for over half of the more than 100 million pieces now housed in the Library of Congress. From its inception and throughout its nearly two-hundred-year history, the Library of Congress has made the collection of Americana its highest priority. Jefferson, as we saw, took advantage of his sojourn in Paris as minister to France to visit the bookstalls, "turning over every book with my own hands, putting by everything which related to America. . . . " Elsewhere in Europe he also actively collected documents relating to the early history of Virginia and the United States, such as transcripts of the papers of the Virginia Company of London, the company that founded and initially governed the oldest English-speaking colony in North America. The Library later acquired the remaining Virginia Company records collected by Jefferson after he sold his library to Congress. The third president's zeal for gathering Americana remains a guiding principle of the Library of Congress in its role as storehouse of the nation's patrimony.

Americana of European provenance includes some of the rarest treasures in the Library's collections. One might argue that the Library's premier example of European Americana is Martin Waldseemüller's *Cosmographiae introductio* of 1507, in which the word "America" appeared in print for the first time. The Rare Book Division's Thacher Collection contains three pre-1510 editions of this work in which Waldseemüller made the fateful error of crediting the discovery of the "fourth continent" to Amerigo Vespucci, whose namesake the nation thereby became.

But before the creation of the name came the discovery of "America," and hence the argument for the *Columbus Codex (Book of Privileges)* of 1502 as our earliest piece of European Americana. In the codex the Spanish crown promised, among other things, that Columbus would be governor of any lands he could discover. The Library of Congress possesses one of four original copies of the *Columbus Codex*—the only copy that includes the Papal Bull of 1493 concerning the New World. The Library also holds the rare manuscript *Copia de littere mandate par Anzolo Trevisan* (1501–3), containing the second account of Columbus's voyages to the New World.

A complete catalog of the Library's holdings of logs, diaries, correspondence, treaties, maps, atlases, and artifacts dating to the age of European exploration and conquest of the Americas would fill volumes. In 1898, the newly created Manuscript Division acquired Benjamin Franklin Stevens's collection of facsimiles and transcripts of British manuscripts. The importance of these European archival

American photographer Frances Benjamin Johnston captured the Lumière brothers, pioneers in the film industry, during a luggage inspection at the French border (1905). *(Frances Benjamin Johnston Collection, Prints and Photographs Division)*

resources for the study of American history led Librarian of Congress Herbert Putnam to initiate in 1905 the Foreign Copying Program. Private donations from James B. Wilbur in 1925 and from John D. Rockefeller, Jr., in 1927 permitted the program to expand. Material from European archives and libraries has since been selected on the basis of its relevance to the history of America and has been reproduced in transcripts, photostats, or microformat. Strongly represented are historical records of European exploration of the New World, of early settlement history, of colonies, of European participation in the American Revolution, and later, of diplomatic and cultural relations between Europe and the United States. Archives from England, France, and Spain have been the main focus of this program. Materials have also been collected from Italy, Germany, the Netherlands, and Russia.

Gifts of original materials from private collectors Edward S. Harkness in 1927 and Hans P. Kraus in 1969 brought to the Library invaluable documents concerning the early Spanish and Portuguese explorations of—and settlements in—the Americas. The Harkness Collection alone includes nearly 4,500 folios of documents from the first two centuries of Spanish rule in Mexico and Peru. The Mexican documents pertain mostly to the conquistador Hernando Cortés and his family, and the Peruvian manuscripts include materials on Francisco Pizarro. The Spanish conquest and subsequent treatment of the native American populations were described in exhaustive detail by the contemporary historian and missionary, Bartolomé de las Casas (1474–1566), known as "Protector of the Indians." The Rare Book and Special Collections Division has custody of several sixteenth- and seventeenth-century editions of Las Casas's works, including his *Brevissima relacion de la destrvycion de las Indias.* Among the Library's most prized Spanish maps of exploration is one of two extant original copies of Diego Gutierrez's map of 1562, where the name "California" appeared for the first time.

Perhaps the finest bibliographic description of America from the period 1492–1551 is Henry Harrisse's *Bibliotheca Americana vetustissima* (1866), which focuses on the voyages of Columbus, John and Sebastian Cabot, Jacques Cartier, and other early explorers. The Library's Harrisse Collection includes the author's personal, annotated copies of this and other works, as well as one of the most valuable examples of French Americana—the original vellum manuscript map of northeastern North America drawn in the winter of 1606–7 by the explorer Samuel de Champlain himself. The detailed map accurately located native American villages, as confirmed by recent archaeological finds. Among the Library's many rare sixteenth-century pieces relating to the voyages of Cartier and Champlain, one finds such enticing titles as: *A shorte and briefe narration of the nauigation made by the commandement of the king of France, to the islands of Canada, Hochelaga, Saguenay, and diuers others which are now called New France, with the particulars customes, and maners of the inhabitants therein* (London, 1600). A work of special anthropological and linguistic interest is *Les voyages de la Nouvelle France occidentale, dicte Canada, faits par le Sr de Champlain Xainctongeois . . .* (Paris, 1632), which includes translations of French religious texts into the native Huron and Montagnais languages.

The Library holds a vast and diverse collection of material relating to the English exploration and colonization of America. A noteworthy example is the 1612 engraving of Captain John Smith's amazingly accurate map of the western shore of Chesapeake Bay. Another treasure is Thomas Jefferson's personal copy of transcripts of the *Records of the Virginia Company of London*, which describe in poignant detail the daily hardships encountered by northern Europeans transplanted to the swampy wilderness at Jamestown.

Among the many British histories of the colonies in Jefferson's collection, transferred to the Library of Congress in 1815, one finds a first edition (1738) of Sir William Keith's *The History of the British Plantations in America . . .* , published in London by the Society for the Encouragement of Learning. Providing unique insight into the British administration of the American colonies, the Sir Thomas Phillipps and the George Chalmers manuscript collections include inter alia the journals of the Council of Foreign Plantations, accounts of colonial revenues, and letters, orders, laws, and notes about the jurisdiction of the Church of England.

The Library of Congress also possesses important materials on Central European settlers in Colonial America. An interesting item with these roots is Augustine Herrman's map *Virginia and Maryland as it is planted and inhabited this present year 1670 surveyed and exactly drawn by the only labor & endeavor of Augustine Herrman bohemiensis.* Herrman was a Czech émigré who came to America via Holland.

Another part of the Library's holdings in Central European Americana concerns the Ephrata religious community. Established in the 1730s in Lancaster County, Pennsylvania, Ephrata is a significant chapter of the early German experience in America. The community's founder, the poet, composer, and radical Pietist Johann Conrad Beissel (1690–1763), emigrated to America in the 1720s in search of a place where he could put his religious theories into practice. In the eighteenth century Ephrata was renowned for its scriptorium in which the sisters of the cloister were trained to illuminate music manuscripts and to

Jón Ólafsson. *Alaska; Lýsing á landi og landskostum* (Washington, 1875). Description of Alaska by an Icelandic traveler who wished to found an Icelandic colony there. President Grant's approval of the idea led to this unique publication of the Government Printing Office in the Icelandic language. (*Rare Book and Special Collections Division*)

write the distinctive German Fraktur script, providing one of the earliest examples of its use in America. Beissel, who composed hymns and other religious music, also established a singing school in the community, whose performances drew audiences from elsewhere in Pennsylvania and which, it is said, on occasion included Benjamin Franklin.

The Library's Music Division holds many fine examples of the Ephrata community's illuminated music manuscripts, as well as exceptional works in Fraktur. Foremost among these is the *Ephrata Codex*, which contains "Das Gesäng der einsamen Turtel-Taube" (The Song of the Lonely Turtle Dove) (1746), one of the earliest pieces of German music written in America.

The Library is richly endowed with European Americana relating to the War of Independence. From the British perspective, for example, the Richard Howe Collection contains a map of the Chesapeake Bay region, locating British headquarters and landing sites. As commander of the British fleet in North America, Howe may have consulted this very map in planning military strategy during the early years of the war. The John Hills Collection contains maps used by Sir Henry Clinton, commander in chief of British military operations between 1778 and 1781. In the Library's Faden Collection, researchers will find detailed maps depicting the campaigns of Clinton and his compatriots Sir William Howe, Charles Cornwallis, and John Burgoyne. An important piece of English-German Americana, housed in the Manuscript Division, is the original treaty between the Duke of Brunswick and Great Britain (1776), providing for a specified number of the duke's troops for service in America.

European military advisers and commanders played a pivotal role in the Revolutionary War, and the names Lafayette, von Steuben, Kościuszko, Pułaski, and Rochambeau hold permanent places in the pantheon of American national heroes. The letters of these and other European officers to the likes of Washington, Jefferson, Madison, and Hancock are among the Library's most treasured manuscripts. The following extract from Washington's letter welcoming Kościuszko back to the United States in 1797 reveals the founding fathers' gratitude to their European comrades-in-arms:

Having just been informed of your safe arrival in America, I was on the point of writing you a congratulatory letter on the occasion, welcoming you to the land whose liberties you had been so instrumental in establishing. . . . no one has a higher respect, and veneration for your character than I have; or one who more sincerely wished, during your arduous struggle in the cause of liberty and your country, that it might be crowned with Success.

The title page to the music manuscript *Paradisisches Wunder-Spiel* . . . (Ephrata, Pennsylvania, 1754), is a fine example of the intricate German Fraktur script used at the Ephrata religious community. *(Music Division)*

Paradisisches Wunder-Spiel,

Welches sich

In diesen letzten Zeiten und Tagen
In denen Abend-Ländischen Welt-Theilen als ein Vor-
spiel der neuen Welt hervor gethan. Bestehende
In einer gantz neuen und ungemeinen Sing-
Art auf Weise der Englischen und himm-
lischen Chören eingerichtet.

Da dann das Lied Mosis und des Lamms, wie auch das hohe Lied Salomonis samt noch mehrern Zeugnüssen aus der Bibel und andern Heiligen
in liebliche Melodyen gebracht. Wobey nicht weniger der Zuruf der
Braut des Lamms, sammt der Zubereitung auf den herrlichen
Hochzeit-Tag trefflich Præfigurirt wird.

Alles nach Englischen Chören Gesangs-Weise mit viel Mühe und grosem Fleiß
ausgefertiget von einem

Friedsamen,

Der sonst in dieser Welt weder Namen noch Titul suchet.

EPHRATÆ Sumptibus Societatis: 1754.

MOT' I DYTE

Dél per Jave.

Kombi

SECOND YEAR

Published Weekly.

"KOMBI" eshte mprognes i interésavé kombetaré te Shciptarevé édhé i vétemi organ i tyré n' Amérike.

The "KOMBI", (The Nation) is devoted to the national interests of the Albanians and is their only organ in America.

No. 79 — BOSTON, MASS., March 20, 1908. — Vol. III.

Una lettera.

Palazzo Adriano, 4 Febb., 1908.

Illmo Sig. Direttore,

Pervenutomi con la posta di ieri il „Kombi" diretto dalla S. V., mi affretto rispondere, ringraziandola, insieme al Chiarissimo Prof. Carnesi, per gli encomù prodigatimi, immeritevolonente. --Le dico, Sig. Direttore, che per una trentina di anni, mi consacrai a serivere composizioni albanesi, col solo intendimento di rendere un servizio alla nazionalità e null' altro-- Non credo che in me risieda l'anima del poeta, ma di un umile verseggiatore, che, buttato nell' ozio e nell' oblio di un paesello, si diletta a forzare gli affezionati ed ardenti Shciptari a rimembrare gli usi, i costumi e lo spirito dei nostri nobili, ma sventurati proavi, i quali, da fuorusciti, seppero per cinque secoli, mantenere con rara tenacia, e schivarono di confondersi con gl' inpigeni. Ad onta di ciô, il pericolo è imminente. Ció che si è tramandato sino ai nostri giorni, parmi che tosto voglia scomparire, se l' attività e la potenza delle opere e della penna, non sapranno vivificare nelle vene quel sangue intiepidito; Bisogna dirlo con dolore, in molti dei nostri connazionali, i quali, più che in alto si estollono nelle dignità, piú si allontanano dal sentimento e dall' amore patriottico. É sacro dovere di chi sa e può, lottare per la conservazione delle colonie e per l' autonomia della madre patria. Ma, per arrivare atanto, avremmo bisogno di scuole, collegi ed asili infantili per l' insegnamento razionale della nostro lingua e per quella instruzione ed educazione, che dovrebbero sempre avere il miraggio del sentimento albanese.

Educato cosi la tenera prole, per conseguenza, sorgerebbero più forte il sentimento albanese nella famiglia avvenire.

A che valgono i riti, la liturgia chiesiastica, quando è scomparsa la nostra lingua? Noi di greco non abbiamo che il rito soltanto, non il sangue – quindi ci preme piû la lingua che il rito. Sono piú considerate albanesi le colonie dove scomparve la lingua? Bronte, Gran Michele, S. Angelo Muxaro e piú tardi Mezroiuso, avranno più affetto per la patria lontana, quando hanno perduto usi, costumi e lingua?

La lingua ed il rito, entrambi ·é veroformano una gran forza, ma, disgiunti, facilmente si abbattono da chi ha interesse farci scomparire. Ed io parlo franco, signor direttore. E sommo delitto, ad es., vedere ancora il nostro Seminario di Palermo Greco-Albanese di nome, senza una catedra per la lingua degli avi, quando poi si sperpera il danaro per futili insegnamento che a nulla approdano.

Quando, in tutte le nostre colonie la lingua era popolare, quando le commicazioni ed il commercio erano pure rari e quando raro l' infiltramento del siculo dialetto, forse allora non ocorreva l' insegnamento della lingua letteraria. Ma oggi il dilagare delle scuole elementari in ogni citta, paesello e borgate ha fatta si che i teneri bambini che escono di essa, lontani dalla mamuna, ritornano per non piú parlare l' albanese, anche per la forte ragione di accudire ai compiti da riportare al maestro.

Ecco il vero e precipuo danno al quale si dovrebbe cercare con tutti i mezzi un riparo, ed il riparo dovrebbe nascere dal Governo, il quale dovrebbe dare scuole albanesi nei paesi Albanesi d' Italia.

Avrei molto da dire. Ma per ora mi fermo e le accludo 4 poesiette copiate al volume dal proi. Tomase Carnesi.

La essequio e la ringrazio sempre.

Suo dev·mo

F. Crispi Glaviano.

Te rat' é Shciperise.

Luft' é Chérchixit mé Ushterine.

Te Hene ce shkoj me 3 te Shkurtit shume ushtéri u nis nga Korcha per ne Monastir, keshtu thane, po kur ndajnat hére muarrme vésh nga gnéres ce ardhe préj Xvéxdé, sé ajo ushteri ce dolli ishté derguar kunder Chérchixit dhé shokevé tij. Tradhetia cenké bere nga Korcha: ushteri mé téjshkrim dolli édhé nga Bilishti, po nuk harriu ghe. Chérchixi mé shoket ishté per m'at' ane te Pilurit, midis Pilurit é Xvéxdes ner pllajat é malit Ivan. Lufta u nis édhé fundi i saj ishté ce, gne nga shoket é Chérchixit u vra (thuhét sé ishté i Krishtére) dy ushtetare te plagosur i shpune ne Bilisht. Chérchixi mé shoket shpetuan, sé sikunder thuhét paska cene vétem mé 9 shoke, édhé réxik do ish po t'a rréthonin ushterite. Per te vrarin é kesaj chété u muarr vésh sé cenka Bulgar nga pshatrat é Kuréshtes. Cévéria pastaj hapı fjale, sé chéta ce u godit mé ushterine ishté chéte Bulgaresh, po keto jane pofka te programit Hilmiut, tsili ka dhene urdher te shtrenguar ce kur te godités ushteria mé chéta Shcipetaresh te mos trégojne sé luftuan mé Shcipetare. Ghithe keto ce te mos marrine vésh konsujte é te huajte, sé ka chéta kombetaré te Shcipetarevé. E pastaj s' ka politike, thone, Hilmi pashaj!!

G. C.

Traximé kombetaré nde kaxa te Permétit.

Djé ardhe gnéres nga Perméti é na thane, sé traximé fort te medha po behén ne Laberi, Chameri dhé ne Dangelli. Valiu i Janines naten mê shume é shkon ne télégrafane sé sa ne shtepi. Kane bastisur shume hére pshatra ne Laberi édhé shume arme é fishéke ghétne. Shume véta kane dale malévét: Cévéria po shtrengon far' é fisne é kachakevé, pas programit poshter ce ka. Nga keto shtrengimé asghe s' fiton cévéria, pervéch sé nga frika é mundimévé ce shohim nga cévéria, gnérexia marrin syte dhé kembet édhé léne shtepite é fémijen, é kesisoj dalin ner malét, d. m. th. sé céveria ka nisur mé gne fare pro grami ce t'a madhogne chestjén kombetare te Shcipetarevé. Tani ka nisur é dergon me ch'do pshat ushte are te rign ce ka sjélle nga Anadolli mé mjékera, si thame mé siper ner thémat é para. Po ch' dobi do te bjére kjo fare méthodé? Ajo véte s'é di, po névé shigur mundim t'a thomi. Vendi mê téper égersohét, gnérexit Shcipetare Musulmane, duké pare gne ghe te tille te cévérise, kupetojne édhé ata me te paditurit sé Sulltani s' paska mbésim ner Musulmanet é Rumélise, dhé perandaj sjéll Anadollake, keshtu é humbasin dhé ate te pake simpathi ce kane me kryén é Halifatit d. m. th. ata te béses ce kish ghér me sot pas véthés saj, Cévéria, édhé ata pasketaj do te behén gherpign per ate. Sot per sot scéne théatrojé eshte Shciperia, ku lohét gne drame fort é habichimé. Chestja shcipetaré é ka bere dhé Stambolle ce te dridhét.

Vétem gne ghe na duhét ndihmes né Shcipetarevé sot. Na lypsét ce keta te véghelit si Bulgari, Serbi, Mal' i Xi é Grécia ce réthojne Turcine te mos bejne nogne fare lidhjé micesié mé Turcine é t'a léne ne prehjé, édhé pastaj névé na ghén dem i math, sé duké chkujdésur Turcia nga ata armic, do muntgne me liruar é mé fuci me te madhé te na bjére kemba kembes pas. Po sikuuder sot shohim nde cark te politikes Evropes ce xuri te turbellohét carku i pacese é i bashkimit midis tsa fucivé, mundim mé shiguri te thomi sé véghelise nuk u jép dore te pajtojne mé Turcine, per nga ndogne grusht mé krundé, andaj kémi shprése te madhé sé ky vit i 1908 do te shenogne ne Istori tsa facé te saj mé trimeri te Shcipetarevé. O burra ô djémi ô burrani ô Shcipetare! kohe mê te mire sé sot nuke ka per te ardhur. O velléxer Gége! yvé ch' beni valle? Tunduni pake mos flini, mos mbyllini syte, mos kthéni koken me gn'ane, po mérrni armet per liri te atdhéut, i tsili po tsopetonét nga armicte.

Korche 11 Shkurt, 1908. G. C.

Aferdita é Shciperise.

Kur gne udhetar duké hétsur ne hérresire te nates shéh yllin „Aferdita" te chfacét ne ciéll, i mbushét xémra plot gas dhé plot shprése, sé pas atij ylli te vogel do te vigne gne m'i math dhé m'i ndrichim per te ndrichuar ghithe boten, do te vije djélli, tsili mbush gas, shprése dhé deshire ch'do xémer gnérexie.

Keshtu édhé Shcipetari sot shéh gne léhtesi ne xémer te tija édhé pa durim prét te shohe dhé ay ate yll ac te bukur, ate shegne te perparimit t'i chfacét ner syt' é tija ate te tsilin s' ka patur fatbardhesine t'a shekogne ketu é kacé shékuj me pare.

Prét pa durim ate dite ce te shekoje te parin prift Shcipetar ce enderohéj t'a shikoje kace vjét me pare, é prét mé pa durim dhé mé gas te math sé é di fort mire ce ky eshte udhe refégnes i lirise édhé pasketaj do te shohe ate ce i desheron xémra atij „lirin' é memedhéut".

Velléxer Shcipetare,

Pérendia, beresi i ghithe gnérexise dhé i natyres, duké pare te keciat, te ligat dhé te paudhetat ce po héc kombi Shcipetar nga an'é armicvé nga an' é rasa xésvé te Fanarit, tsilet mé anen te fése duan te lidhin kete komp kok' é kembe, ce te mundin léhtaxi t'a xapetojne; u mallenghyé shume édhé per kete ghe kaili ne xémer te Shcipetarevé deshiren é vertéte dhé durimin, si édhé shenteria é tij épiskopit rus Platonit i rreféu udhen ce te xére per te sherbyér kete komp i tsili desheron te deghoje porosit' é tija ne ghuhen é vét. Dhé Shcipetaret é vertéte u mblodhe nde Hudson, Mass., édhé bashke mé te Marlboro-jt filluan Shocerine „Ndéri Shcipetar" é tsila do te xére te parin vent ne Istorin' é Shciperise.

Keshtu pra mé pelcim te ghithevé xghodhe gne burre mé méntimé te théllla, mé mesimé te lartra dhé mé atdhétarisme te xjarte per te sherbyér tere Orthodoksine. Xghodhe te ndéruarin Fan Nolin, i tsili me 8 te ketij muaji u dorexua prift préj épiskopit rus ne New York. Xoti Fan Noli eshte i pari prift Shcipetar.

Eshte i pare ce duké léne me gn' ane ghithe gaxét dhé defrimét é djalerise u mvésh ner te xéxa, vuri kamilafne mi kryé, dhé u sal per te sherbyér kombin Shcipetar dhé per te ndrichuar bashkatdhétaret é tij mé ane te shegntit Unghill. Xoti Fan Noli eshte i pari atdhétar, tsili keput xinzhirat é renda te patrikanes duké méshuar shcip. Te lumte ô bir i Shciperise!

Ky i pari prift Shcipetar eshte gne dem i math per armiket t'ane te tsilet ghér ..e djé s' bésonin per te tille ghe; dhé kur i thashe gne Gréku per kete, me tha tsa fjale ce me pikuan ne xémer, me tha keto: „E kur kini bere ghe mé rendesi ce te beni dhé tani, Shocerite t'uaj jane nde buxe te varit"...

Mé xe te forte, i thashe: Tani pa é deghon sé si punojne Shcipetaret, é jo si yvé.

Si u largua Gréku, u méntuash é thashe: Vertét ka te dréjte sido ce thote, sé Shocerite t'ona jane vétem per te dukur dhé jo sich i kerkon névoja mé rendtsi. O burra ô Shcipetare te perpicémi te lidhémi mé dashuri te ghithe tok, te [illegible]dhim me gn' ane merit' é véchauta, sé na ndalojne shume édhé te pervishémi ghithe per te filluar gne Shoceri mé rendesi.

I pelcégn shume fjalet é Malit Ivanit, dhé lipsét te ghithe te perpicémi per te goditur ate cellim. S' ka dyshim ce tere Shcipetaret do t'a pelcéjne kete méndim, tsilevé u desheron xémera per gne ghe te tille.

Te Djéle me 22 te muajit behét é para méshe shcip ne Boston, Mass., Shcipetaret do te xjédhin nga ghithe anet per te deghuar priftin Shcipetar. Kjo dite eshte dite gaxi, dite defrimi, eshte gne krémté é véchante per tere Shcipetaret, dhé kjo dite do shkruhét mé shkrogna te arta ne Istorien é Shciperise.

Brockton, Mass., 17 Mars. Tom. Papa.

Gne radhua i névojshim per Shcipetaret.

Lamouche L: La Bulgarie dans le passé et le présent Paris 1892.

Lavallée Ih. Histoire de l' empire Ottoman. Paris 1855.

Lavelege E De: La peninsule des Balkans Paris 1888.

Lavisse E et Rambaud A: Histoire générale du quatrième siècle à nos jours Paris 1893-1901.

Loiseau Ch. L'Equilibre Adriatique. Paris 1901.

Millingen Frederich (Osman Seifi Bey) La Turquie sous la règne d' Abdul Aziz.-

Martens F. De Die rusische in der orientalischen Trage St. Petersburg 1877.

Mijatovitch. The history of modern Serbia London 1872.

Miklosich Dr. F. Rumanische Undersuchungen I. Istro und Macedo rumanische Sprachedenkmahler Wien 1881

Marmat: Geogr. universelle tom VI.

Marchiano Stanislao: Studi filologici della lingua Pelasgo.

Mignot: Histoire de l'empire Ott. depuis ses origines jusqu'à 1840

Meyer Gustav: Etymologisches Worterbuch der Albanesischen Sprache.

Mille Pièrre: Revue de deux monde 1897

Meyer Gustave Albanesische Gramatik.

Malte-Brun Geograf univ.

Malte-Brun Ann. des voyageurs.

Mantica Giussepe. Scanderbeg poema profano 2d edition 1895.

Marini Cesare: Memoria sui [illegible] della mozze presso gli Albanesi 18[illegible]

Martina De Leonardo: L'a[illegible] Italo-Albanese con canti origi[illegible]

Marmoc Geograf. Univers[illegible]

Masci Angelo: Discorso sull' origine, i costumi e la stato attuale degli Albanesi nel Regno delle Due Sicilie 1847.

Mezzoefanti Giornale delle Due Sicilie 1852 numbre 52.

Misasi Nicola Marito è Sacerdote.

Mitko: Are Albanése Abx. d'Egypte 1878.

Mitko Eftimie Topographie de la district de Korcha.

Monardo Vita G. Castriéta 1591.

Muller J. Albanien etc. 1844.

Nicocles G. De. Albanesium origine et prosapia 1855

Niebuhr Storia Romana vol I pag 53 1846

Nordan Max Paradexes Sociologigues.

Nénitesca J De la Romanii dui Turcia Europeana 1895

Nicolaides Dr C. La Macédoine Berlin 1899

Non doplomate(un) La Question des reformes dans la Turquie d'Europe Paris 1903.

Novicow J Les luttes entre sociétés humaines.

Novicow J La pisibilité du bonheur Paris 1904

Novicow J La Mission d'Italie Milan 1903

Obedenarn Region Danubienne (extrait du dict. encycl. des sciences medicales, publié sous la direct du I r A Dechambre)

(Ka dhé [illegible]).

Perhaps the crown jewel of the Revolutionary War European Americana is the Library's 1,800-piece Rochambeau Collection, which includes the personal correspondence and military maps used by the comte de Rochambeau, commander in chief of the French forces. One of the most noteworthy pieces in the collection is a manuscript atlas showing French encampments during the march from Yorktown to Boston.

The recorded observations—both impressionistic and scientific—of European visitors to the "new" continent represent an important genre of Americana that the Library possesses in abundance. Two of the most enduring and influential examples of this type of literature we owe to the French travelers Alexis de Tocqueville and Michel Guillaume St. Jean de Crèvecoeur. The Library owns the only extant set of the first edition of de Tocqueville's *Democracy in America* with the four volumes still in their original wrappers.

Other rarities are the Library's first editions in French and English of Crèvecoeur's *Letters from an American Farmer*, in which the term "melting pot" was first used to define the "new race of men," the Americans. Also noteworthy is the Library's outstanding collection of manuscripts and original and facsimile maps executed by the influential German cartographer and writer Johann Georg Kohl, who traveled about America during the mid-nineteenth century. Another fine example of European contributions to American studies is *A Theoretical and Practical Grammar of the Ochipwe Language* (1850), written by the Slovenian bishop Frederic Baraga (1797–1868), a linguist and missionary who lived among various native American tribes.

Among the Library's largest holdings in European Americana are the papers of Carl Schurz (1829–1906), arguably the most politically prominent German immigrant to the United States. Crusading journalist, abolitionist, and advocate of civil service reform, Schurz in a protean career served as U.S. minister to Spain, major general in the Union Army, Reconstruction senator from Missouri, and secretary of the interior. His papers total some 24,500 items.

The Library of Congress has extensive holdings of newspapers in various European languages printed in the United States by recent immigrants. They range from the press of large groups like German-Americans and Polish-Americans to publications of small nationalities. To this latter group, for instance, belongs the world's oldest continuously published Albanian newspaper, *Kombi* (The Nation) (1906–9), subsequently called *Dielli* (The Sun), which was published in Boston. Before Albanian independence in 1912, Albanian immigrants to America used this newspaper to learn to read and write their language, the use of which had been forbidden under their Ottoman rulers.

Founded in 1906 as *Kombi* (The Nation) and subsequently (from 1909 on) called *Dielli* (The Sun), this is the world's oldest continually published Albanian-language newspaper. The issue depicted here reports the March 8, 1908, ordination of Fan S. Noli and with it the establishment of the Albanian Orthodox Church of America. Noli provided leadership and promoted Albanian culture and nationalism at a time when Albania was ruled by the Ottoman Turks. (*Serial and Government Publications Division*)

To these resources in language, religion, history, and literature, European Americana brings its own flesh-and-blood dimension. The quest for information about European ancestors preoccupies millions of Americans, bringing hundreds of them every week to explore the rich genealogical resources of the Library of Congress. The Local History and Genealogy (LH&G) Reading Room offers more than 10,000 indexes, guides, and reference works and an expert staff to advise readers. Gradually, determined researchers discover that valuable resources await them in other reading rooms throughout the Library.

Unique Library of Congress resources include the Family Name Index (a card file housed in the LH&G Reading Room) and tens of thousands of published genealogies and local history volumes (indexed in Marion J. Kaminkow's *Genealogies in the Library of Congress, a Bibliography* and his *United States Local Histories in the Library of Congress, a Bibliography*). An important recent addition is the CD-ROM index of millions of surnames contained in church records microfilmed throughout Europe by the Church of Latter Day Saints. Other rich sources of church data include the records of the Alaskan Diocese of the Russian Orthodox Church (1700s to 1940) in the Manuscript Division and Cyprien Tanguay's seven-volume *Dictionnaire généalogique des familles Canadiennes depuis la fondation de la colonie jusqu'à nos jours* (1871), a monumental work based primarily on Roman Catholic church records that trace the French origins of virtually all Québecois and, hence, of most Franco-Americans.

Most genealogists are curious to learn about the voyage and the ship that brought their ancestors from Europe. Frequently consulted resources for such information include the pioneering work of P. William Filby, *Passenger and Immigration Lists Bibliography, 1538–1900, Being a Guide to Published Lists of Arrivals in the United States and Canada* (1981); Michael Cassady's *New York Passenger Arrivals, 1849–1868* (1983); and Ira A. Glazier's seven-volume *The Famine Immigrants: Lists of Irish Immigrants Arriving at the Port of New York, 1846–1851* (1983–86).

Another common objective of genealogists is to pinpoint the city or village in Europe from which their ancestors emigrated. Deciphering arcane renderings of place-names in various languages and alphabets brings researchers to consult with experts throughout the Library, and to discover such treasures as Filip Sulimierski's *Słownik geograficzny Królestwa Polskiego i innych krajów* (1880); this fifteen-volume classic provides detailed descriptions of the history, economy, and administrative subordination of communities (and the variant spellings of their names) throughout the vast territory of the former Polish-Lithuanian Commonwealth.

GEORGE KLEINE
PRESENTS
THE COSSACK WHIP

The Cossack Whip. Thomas A. Edison Studios, George Kleine distributor, 1916. A melodrama in which a Cossack whip figures in both injustice and retribution, this silent movie is indicative of the American view of Russian absolutism only one year before the United States joined Russia in World War I against the Central Powers. *(Motion Picture, Broadcasting, and Recorded Sound Division)*

Finally, genealogical research frequently has the goal of identifying a family crest, a link with nobility and the shapers of European history. The Library possesses outstanding collections of European armorials, many with splendid color reproductions of European noble family crests. Johann Siebmacher's seventeenth-century classic, *Grosses Wappenbuch,* provides heraldic information for the nobility of Bavaria, Austria, Hungary, Croatia, Bukovina, the Baltic states, Alsace, and numerous other kingdoms and principalities on the continent. Another indispensable reference is J. B. Rietstap's *Armorial général: contenant la description des armoiries des familles nobles et patriciennes de l'Europe* (1861). The crests and lineage of noble families of the British Isles are described in numerous important works by John Bernard Burke, including *The General Armory of England, Scotland, and Wales: Comprising a Registry of Armorial Bearings* (1884).

Many of the treasures described above might as easily have been labeled American Europeana, for they are the heritage of peoples on both sides of the Atlantic. The Library's collections of American Europeana are unmatched in size and diversity. Among the most interesting works in these collections are those that present the American view of Europe. For historians attempting to trace the development of official American perceptions of Europe, what resource could surpass the Library's papers of the U.S. presidents, secretaries of state, and diplomats? The vast assemblage of the W. Averell Harriman Papers, to cite one collection, covers most aspects of the long and eventful career of one of this century's great statesmen, including his service as ambassador to the Soviet Union and coordinator of the European Recovery Program, known as the Marshall Plan.

Over the centuries, visits to Europe have inspired countless American artists to produce some of their finest works. For example, during his 1926 trip to Europe, George Gershwin composed the opening theme of his masterpiece *An American in Paris*, the original score of which resides in the Library's Gershwin collection. In the composer's own words, "My purpose is to portray the impressions of an American visitor in Paris as he strolls about the city, listens to the various street noises and absorbs the French atmosphere."

The Library offers many other splendid examples of the recurring theme of American encounters with Europe, including Joel Barlow's moving letters to his wife from Lithuania and Poland in which he graphically describes the devastation of Napoleon's Russian campaign; an autographed special edition of Mark Twain's hilarious work *Innocents Abroad;* and rare first editions of the major works of American Anglophile Henry James. Early American films depicting Europe such as the Thomas Edison Studios' unflattering 1916 portrayal of Tsarist Russia, *The Cossack Whip*, distributed by George Kleine, and the Paris papers of Janet Flanner, described earlier, represent other aspects of these materials.

It seems appropriate to conclude this guide by mentioning a special aspect of American Europeana: works of European patriots and artists viewing their troubled homelands from American shores. The Library possesses many examples of this genre, including first editions of the speeches of Hungarian patriot Lajos Kossuth (1851–52). Thomas Masaryk's *Nová Evropa*, was written in Washington in 1918 and is cited above. Vojtěch Preissig's dramatic poster invoking support for the Czech and Slovak war efforts against Austria and Germany during World War I was captioned "Czechoslovaks! Join Our Free Colors!" Chronicling the interchange of ideas, cultures, and individuals that has characterized the relationship between Europe and the United States has been one of the enduring contributions of the European collections of the Library of Congress.

A Czechoslovak First World War poster designed by Vojtěch Preissig, a Czech artist who lived in the United States from 1910 to 1930 and died in 1944 in a German concentration camp. *(Prints and Photographs Division)*

CZECHOSLOVAKS! JOIN

OUR FREE COLORS!

ISSUED BY CZECHOSLOVAK RECRUITING OFFICE, 1 MADISON AVE BUILDING, NEW YORK
DESIGNED AND PRINTED AT THE SCHOOL OF PRINTING AND GRAPHIC ARTS OF
WENTWORTH INSTITUTE, BOSTON, MASS. U.S.A. — WENTWORTH POSTER NO. 1

A Brief Researcher's Guide

The primary function of the Library of Congress is to serve the Congress. In addition, the Library provides service to government agencies, other libraries, scholars, and the general public. All researchers preparing to come to the Library are strongly encouraged to pursue preliminary exploration in appropriate public, academic, or special libraries, so that they can make efficient use of the Library.

The Library of Congress is primarily a research library, not a lending library, and its collections are kept in restricted, closed stacks. Because of this role, the Library's lending is restricted to official borrowers or to interlibrary loans, including those made to government agencies. Under certain conditions, the Library lends material from its collections to other libraries for the use of their readers.

The Library's National Reference Service (NRS) provides information by telephone (202–707–5522 and TDY 202–707–4210). The Reference Service directs incoming calls to the appropriate reading room as necessary. Its staff will also offer research strategy and orientation for researchers planning to come to the Library. After exhausting other resources, researchers can send reference inquiry letters to the National Reference Service, which will forward them to the appropriate reading room for response if NRS is unable to answer the inquiries. Letters should be addressed as follows:

> National Reference Service
> Library of Congress
> Washington, DC 20540–5570

To send a letter directly to a specific reading room, substitute its name for "National Reference Service" and delete the last four digits of the zip code.

THE EUROPEAN COLLECTIONS

As stated earlier in this guide, the Library of Congress does not house "European collections" separately. Upon arrival at the Library, the researcher can begin by consulting the reference librarians of the Humanities and Social Sciences Division in the Library's Main Reading Room. These librarians will assist researchers in learning to use the Library's computer catalog (the Library of Congress Information System, or LOCIS) and the Library's card catalog (which is important for its coverage of older materials). The Main Reading Room also has a reference collection of approximately 50,000 volumes.

If answering a question requires specialized language skills, the researcher may consult with a librarian or specialist in the European or Hispanic Reading Rooms. Each of these reading rooms has its own reference collection for the use of researchers. It may also be useful to visit the Newspaper and Current Period-

Vsia Moskva. (Moscow, 1992). An example of a post-Soviet handbook and guide to Moscow, designed for the Russian and foreign businessperson. Unlike directories from the Soviet period, this guide was partially financed by advertising. *(Russian Reference Collection, European Reading Room)*

ВСЯ МОСКВА
ALL MOSCOW

1992/93

ИНФОРМАЦИОННО-
РЕКЛАМНЫЙ
ЕЖЕГОДНИК

СПУТНИК
ДЕЛОВОГО ЧЕЛОВЕКА

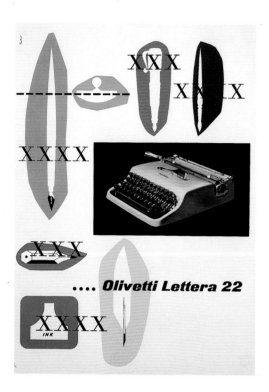

icals Reading Room, which has custody of current periodicals in most European languages, with the exception of current Slavic- and Baltic-language titles, which are found in the European Reading Room.

For materials other than periodicals or books in the general collection, the researcher must visit one of the specialized reading rooms of the Library. Generally these reading rooms have custody of materials based on the format of the materials rather than by their geographic origin. Thus prints are in the Prints and Photographs Reading Room, music scores are in the Performing Arts Reading Room, and so on. One of the primary tasks of a reference librarian at the Library of Congress in assisting a researcher is to know where to refer him or her within this large and complex library. Each reading room offers finding aids, bibliographies, and other reference materials as well as the main computer catalog.

The following is a list of the reading rooms and special collections centers most likely to be of value to a researcher with an interest in Europe:

Business Reference Services. Adams Building, LA 508
European Reference Desk. Jefferson Building, Alcove 7 of LJ 100
Geography and Map Reading Room. Madison Building, LM B01
Hebraic Section. Adams Building, LA 128B
Hispanic Reading Room. Jefferson Building, LJ 205
Law Library Reading Room. Madison Building, LM 201
Local History and Genealogy Reading Room. Jefferson Building, LJ G20
Main Reading Room. Jefferson Building, LJ 100
Manuscript Reading Room. Madison Building, LM 101
Microform Reading Room. Jefferson Building, LJ 107
Motion Picture and Television Reading Room. Madison Building, LM 336
Newspaper and Current Periodical Reading Room. Madison Building, LM 133
Performing Arts Reading Room. Madison Building, LM 336
Prints and Photographs Reading Room. Madison Building, LM 339
Rare Book and Special Collections Reading Room. Jefferson Building, LJ 256
Recorded Sound Reference Center. Madison Building, LM 113
Science Reading Room. Adams Building, LA 508

Most reading rooms have brochures describing their collections, hours of operation, and services that they provide. Such brochures will be mailed to researchers if they call or write the National Reference Service. For general information, researchers should request the brochure *Public Services in the Library of Congress,* which describes the hours and locations of all the Library's reading rooms and special collections centers.

Giovanni Pintori. *Olivetti Lettera 22* (1953), a silkscreen print. Adriano Olivetti commissioned internationally renowned designers to produce posters and advertisements for his firm near Milan. *(Poster Collection, Prints and Photographs Division)*